This Book Belongs To..

....

....

....

....

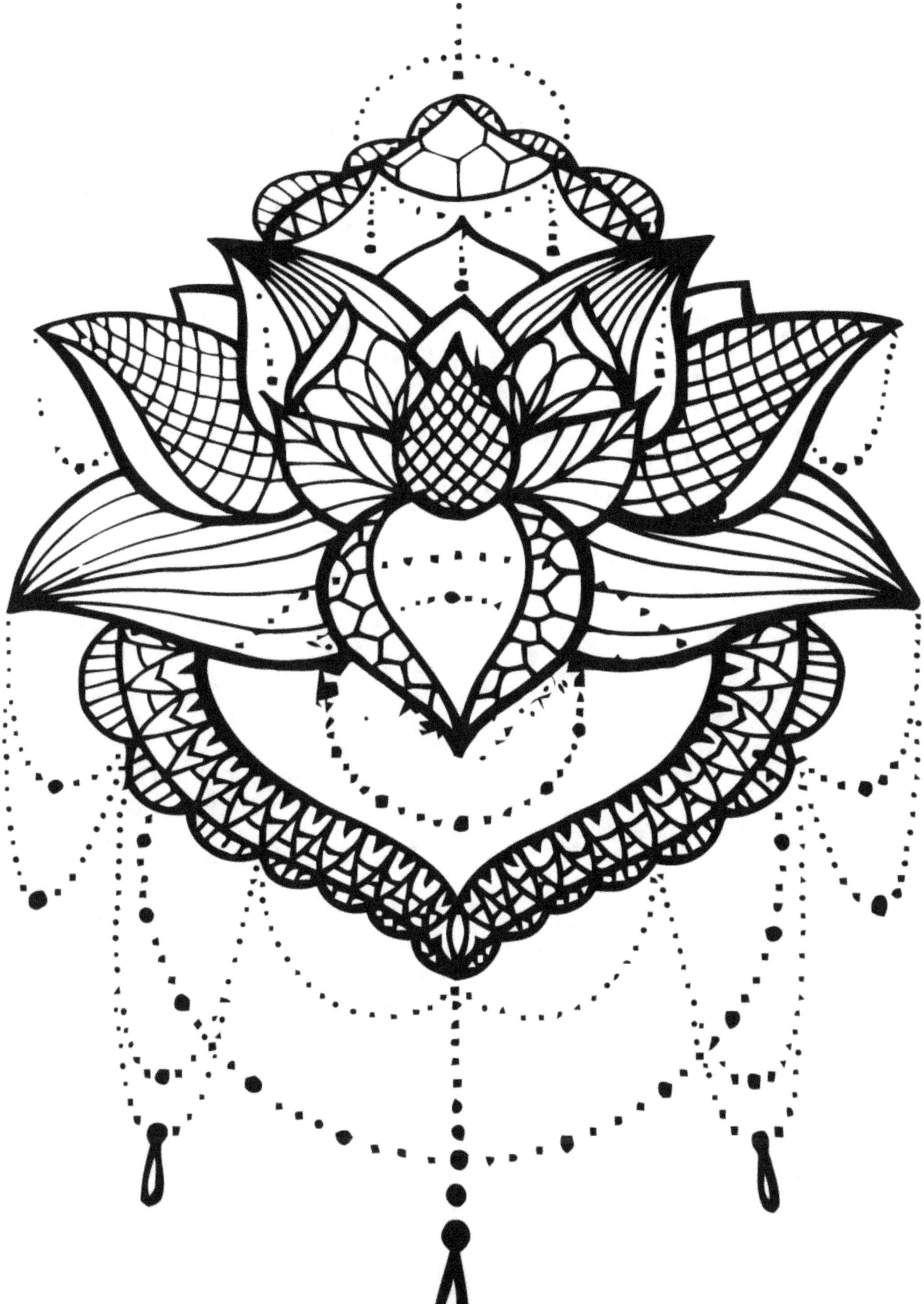

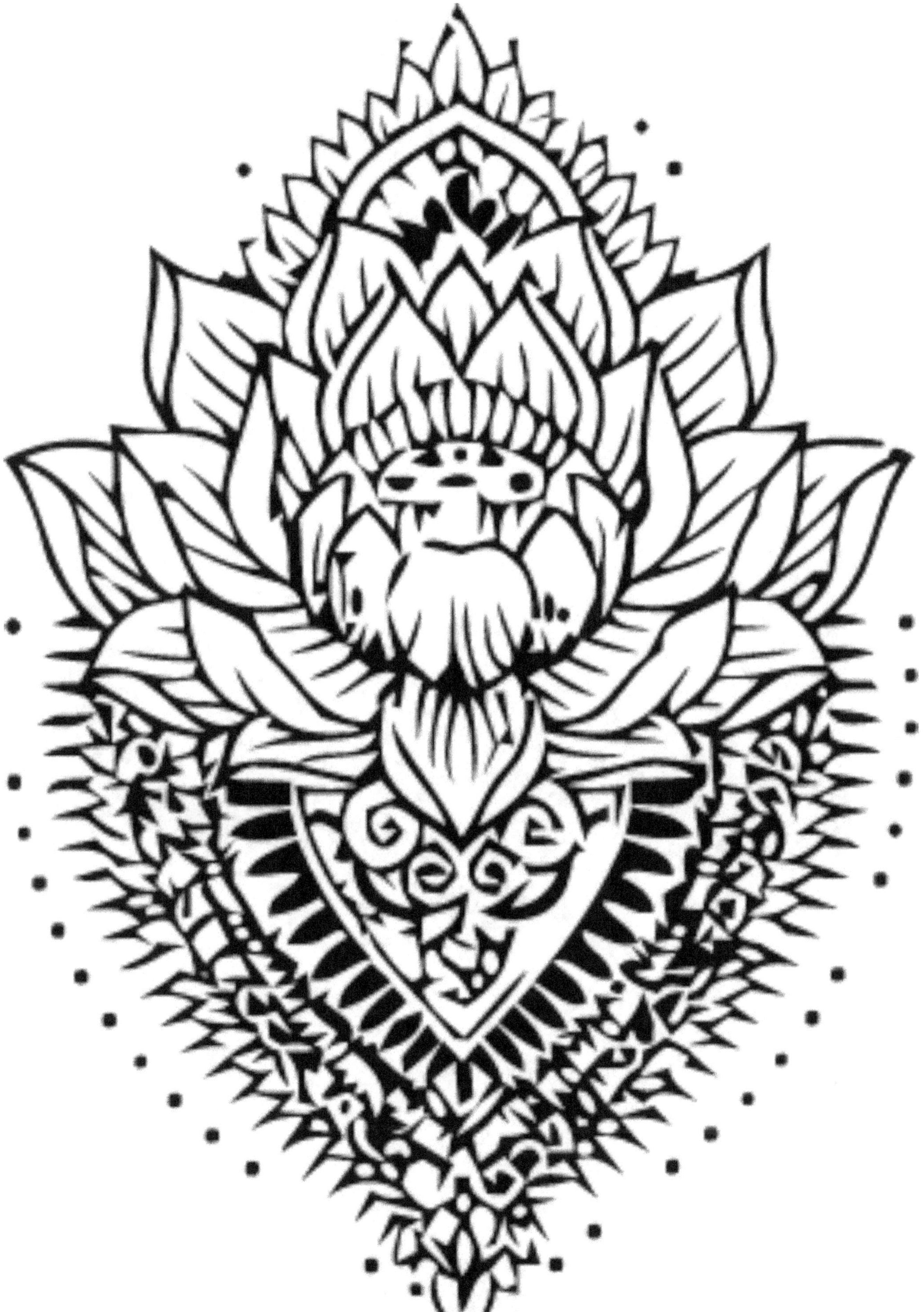

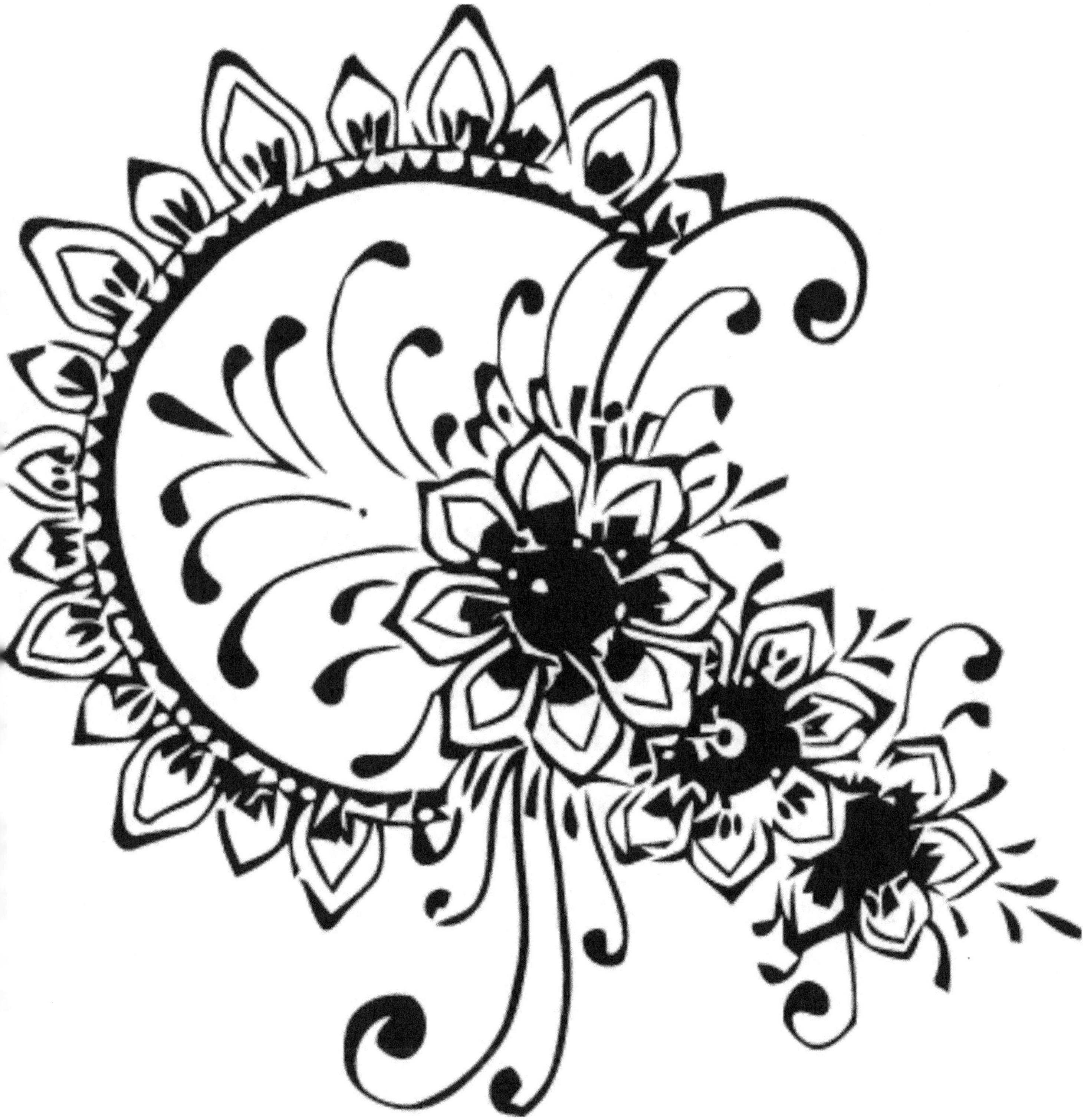

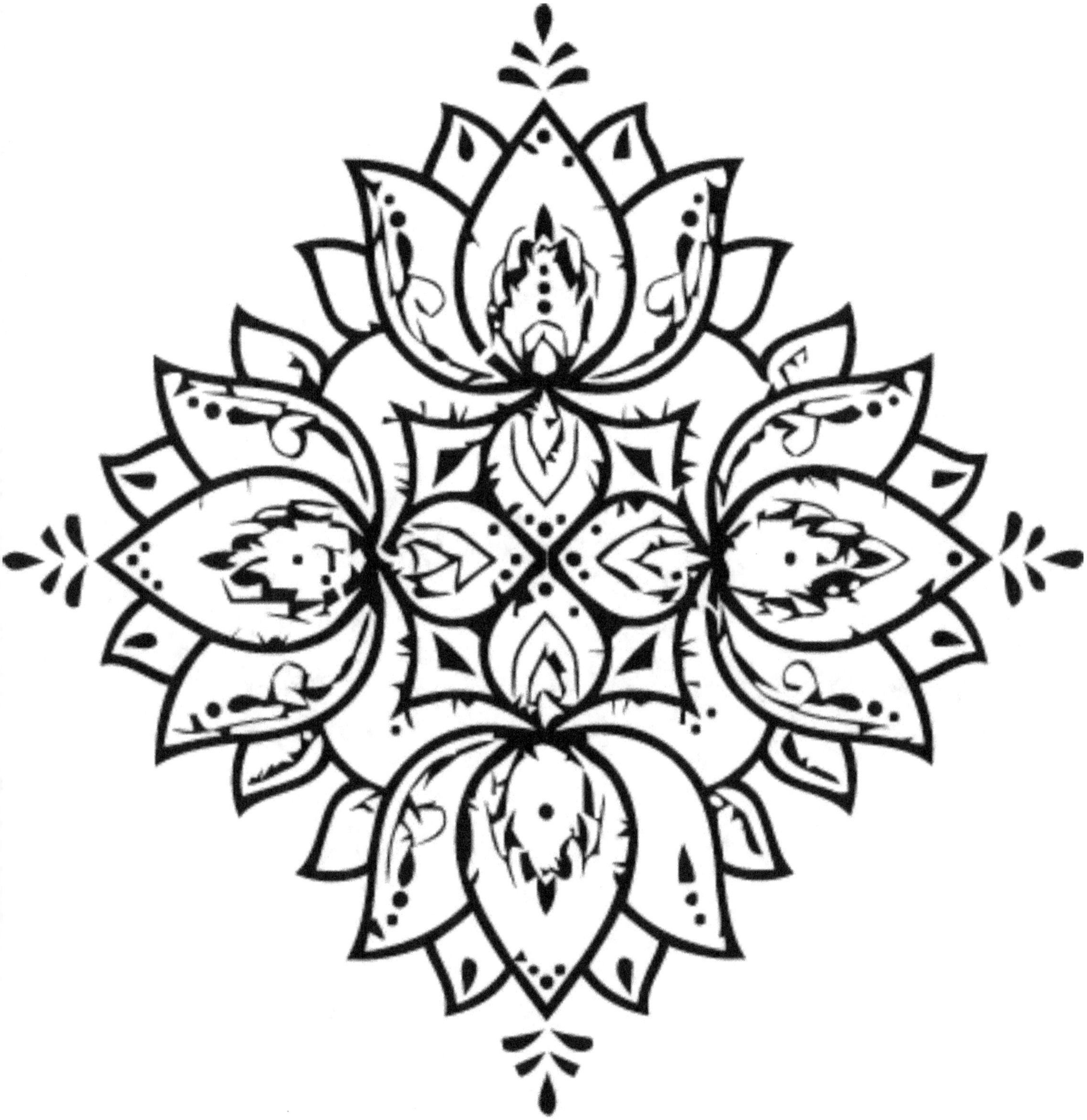

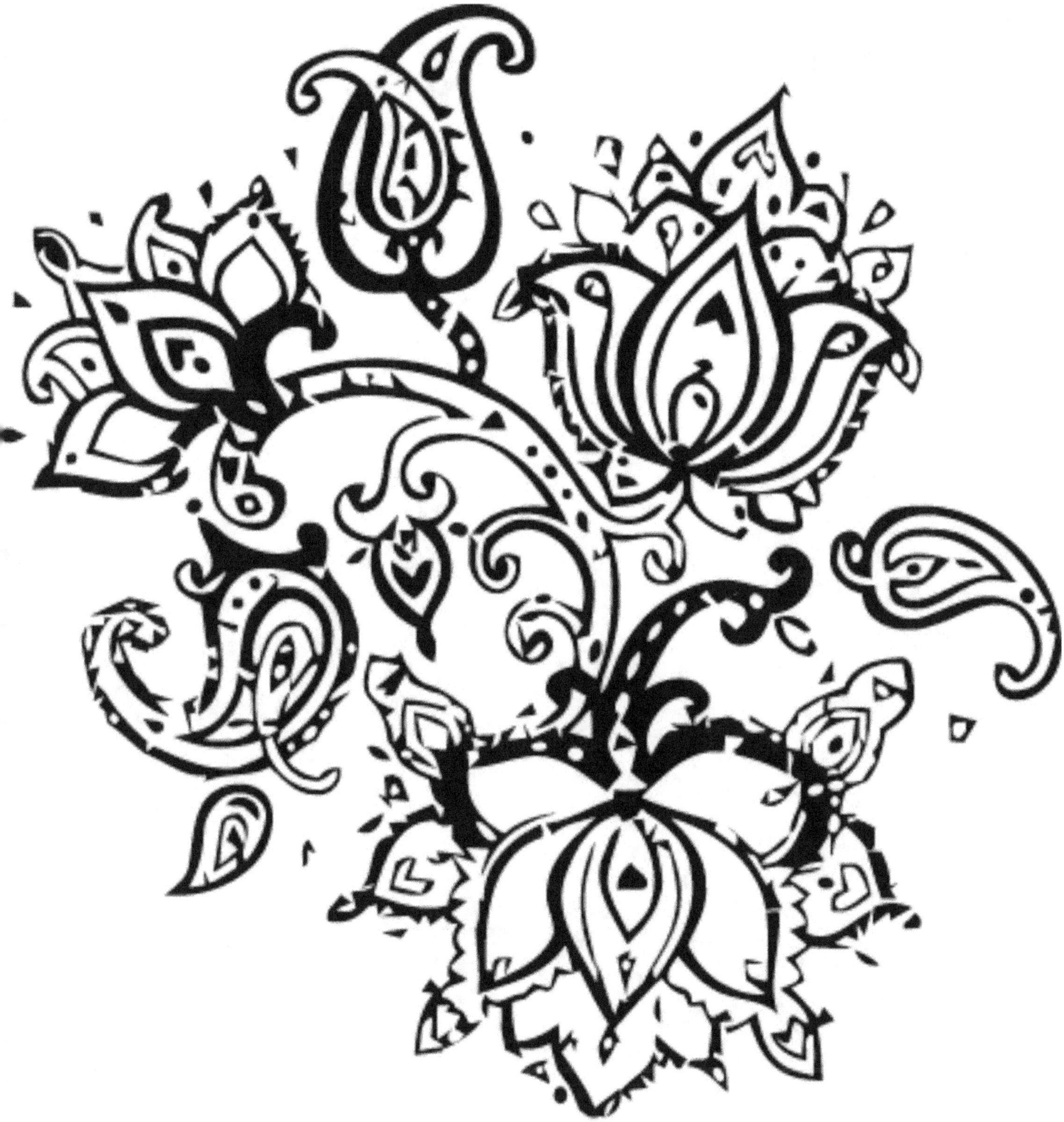

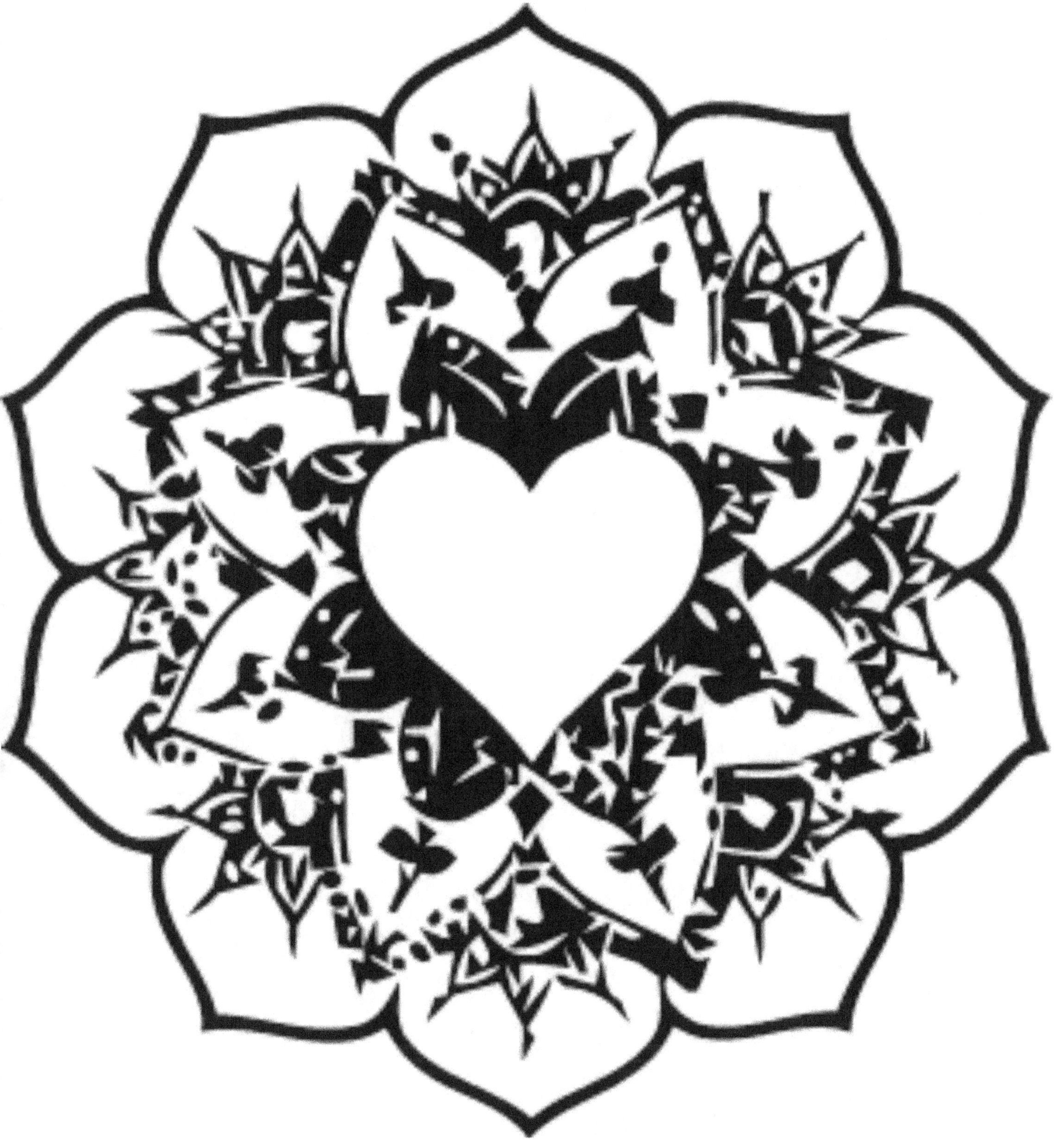

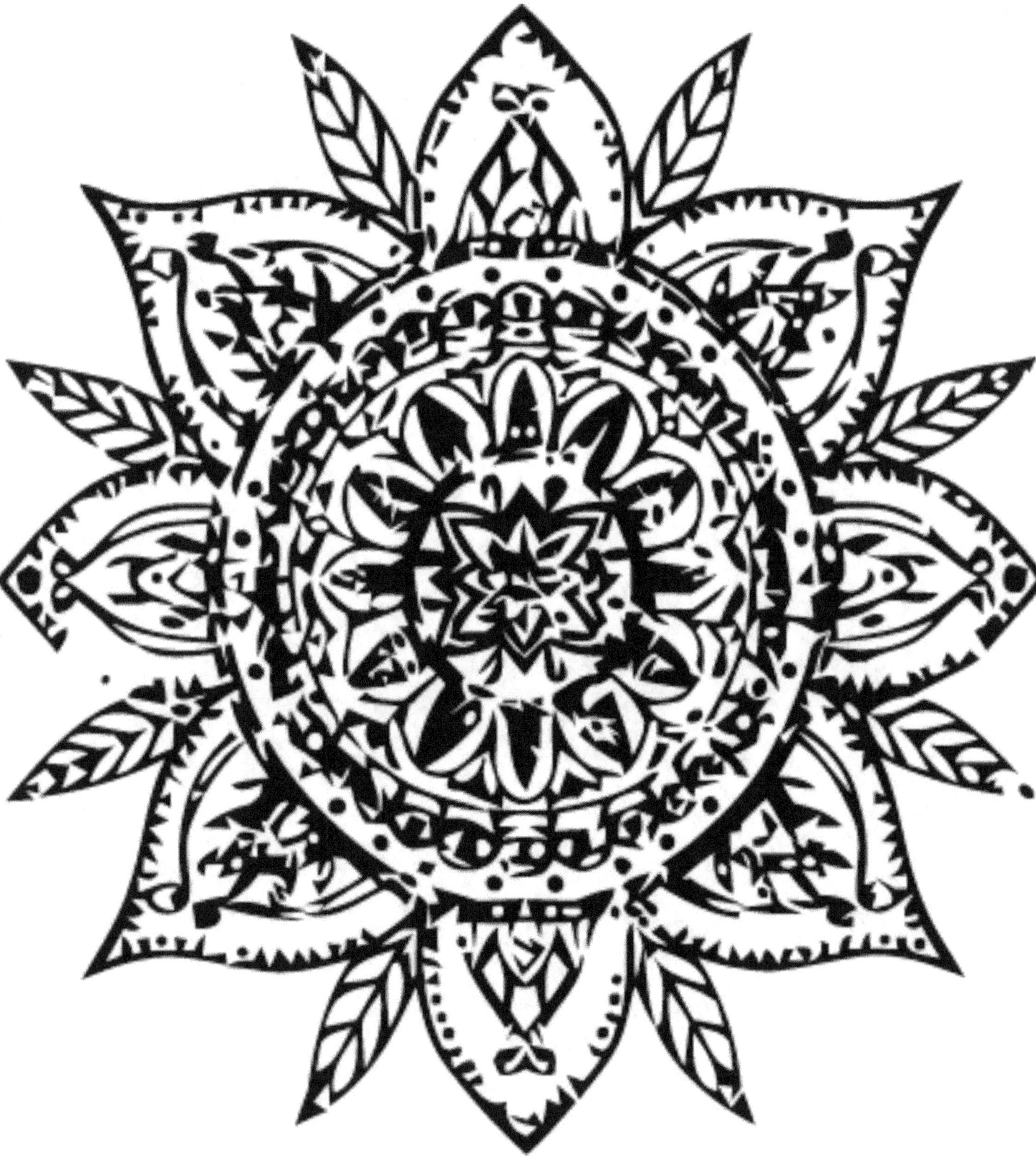

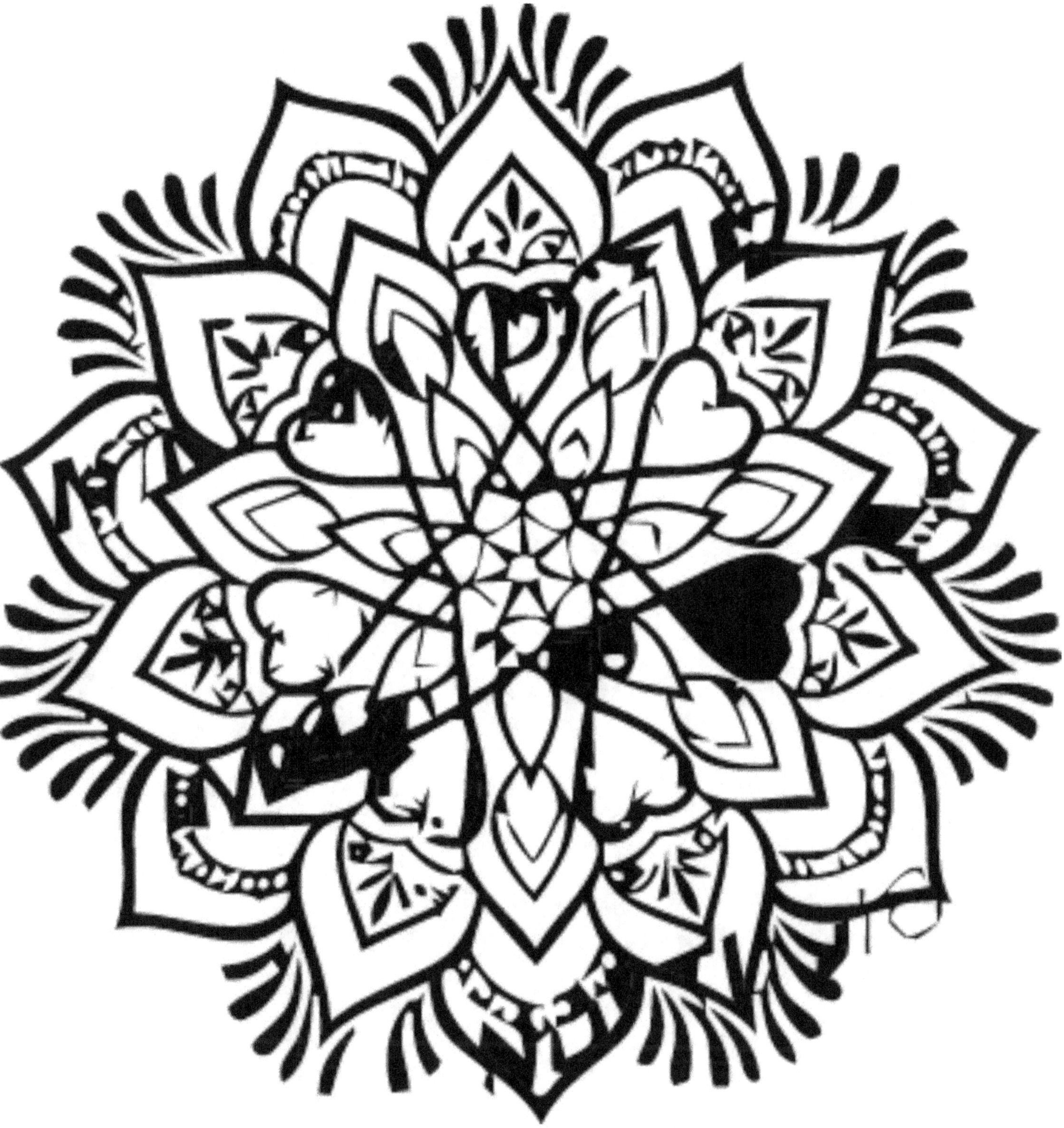

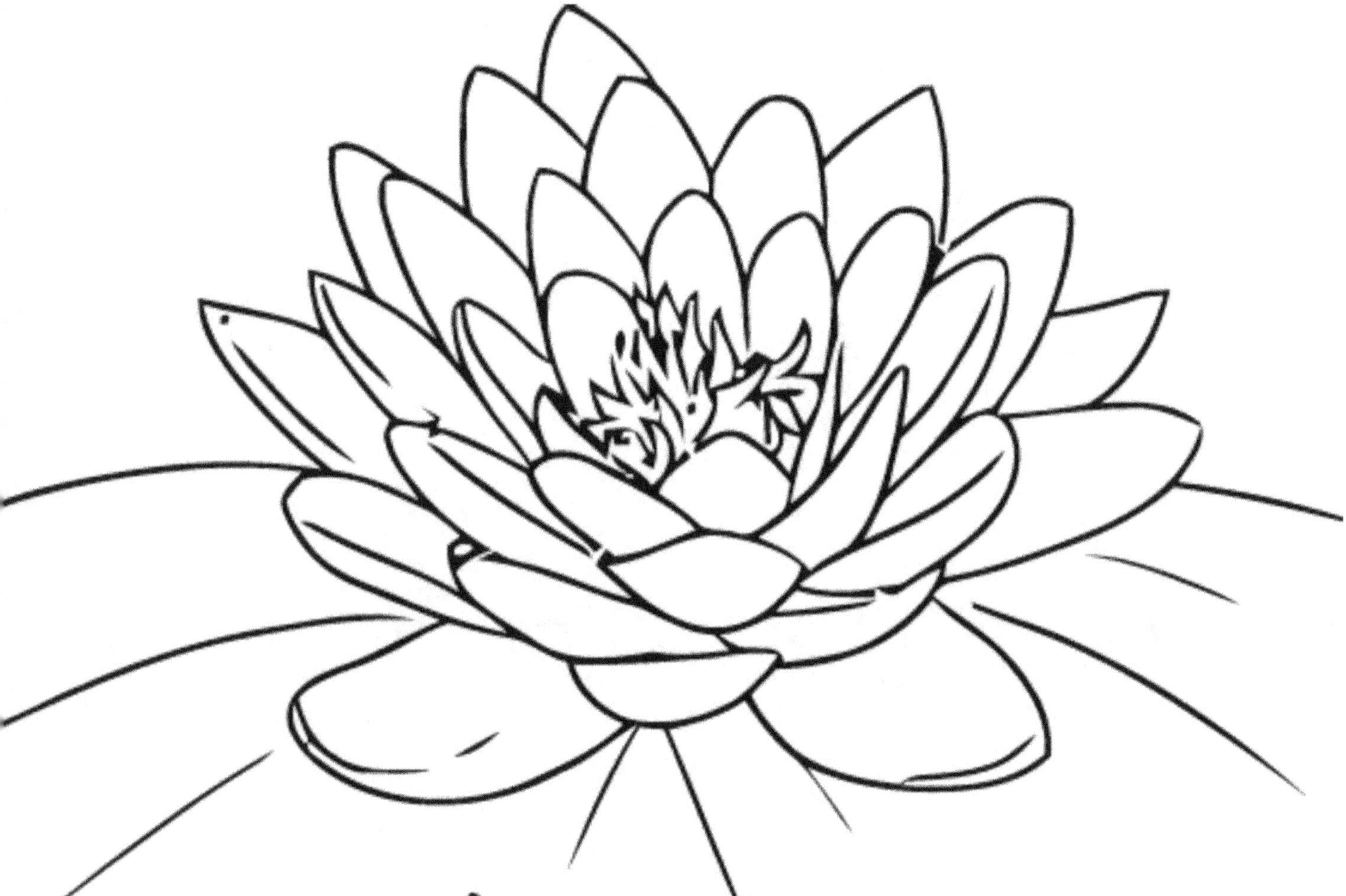

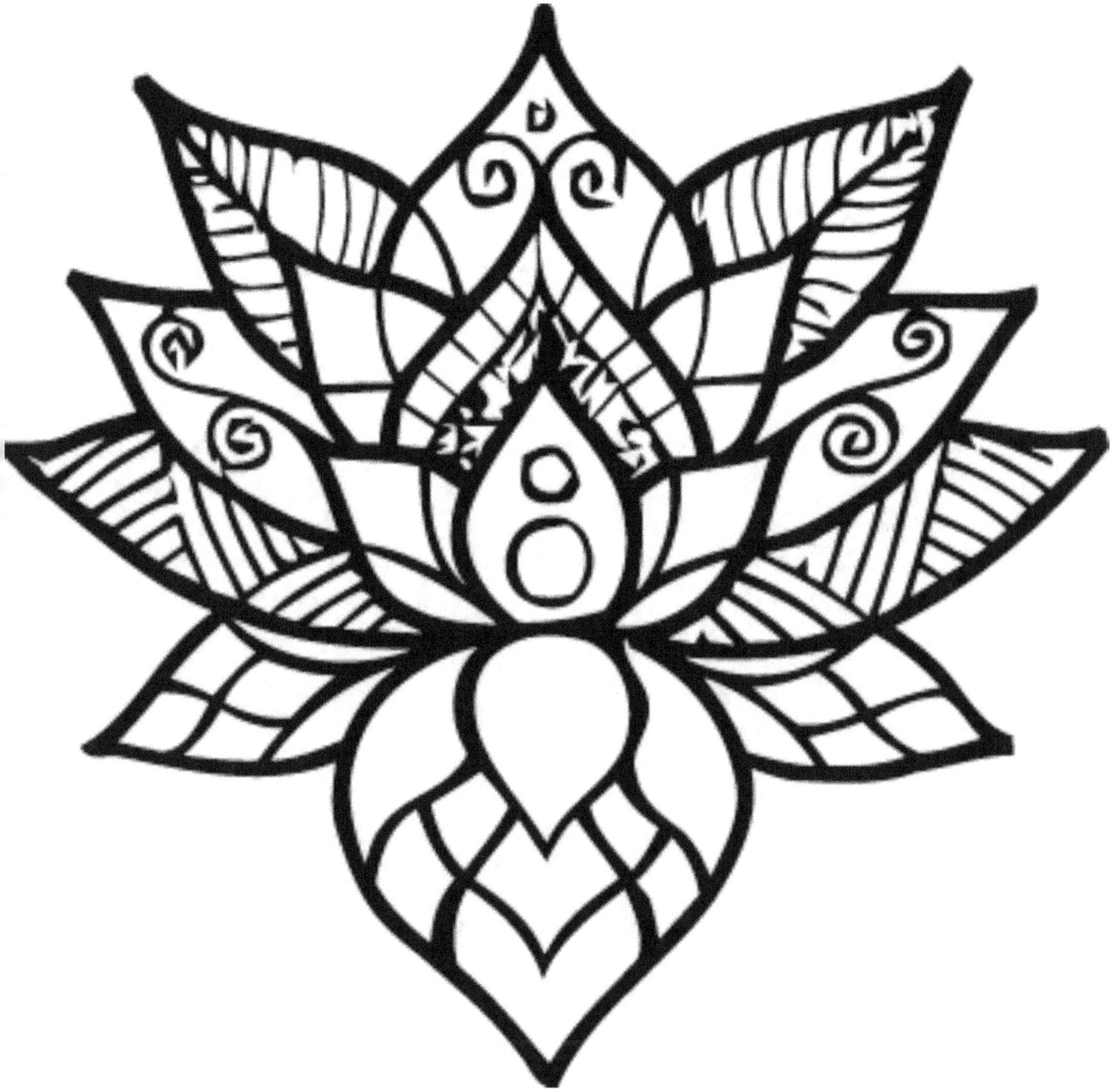

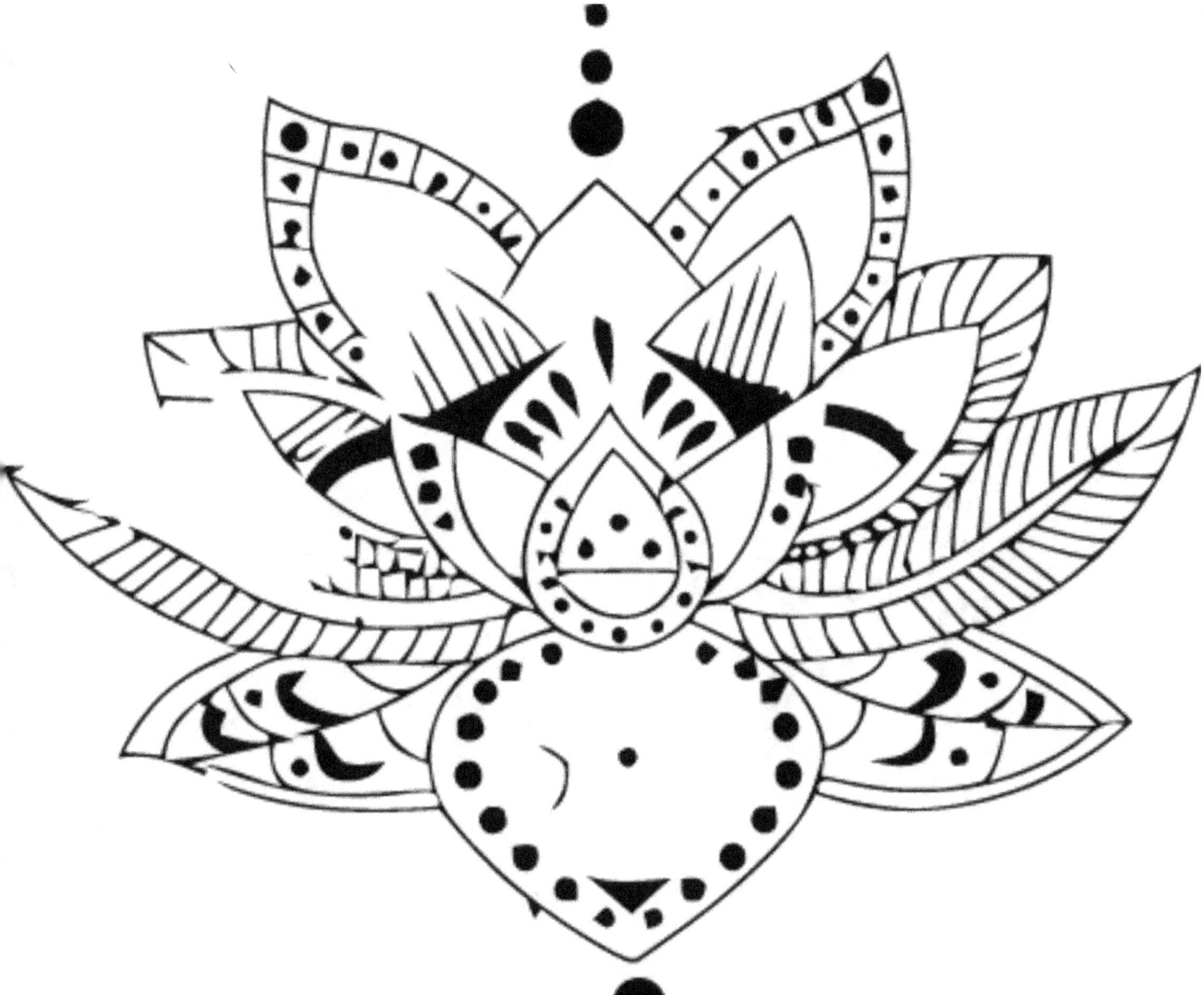

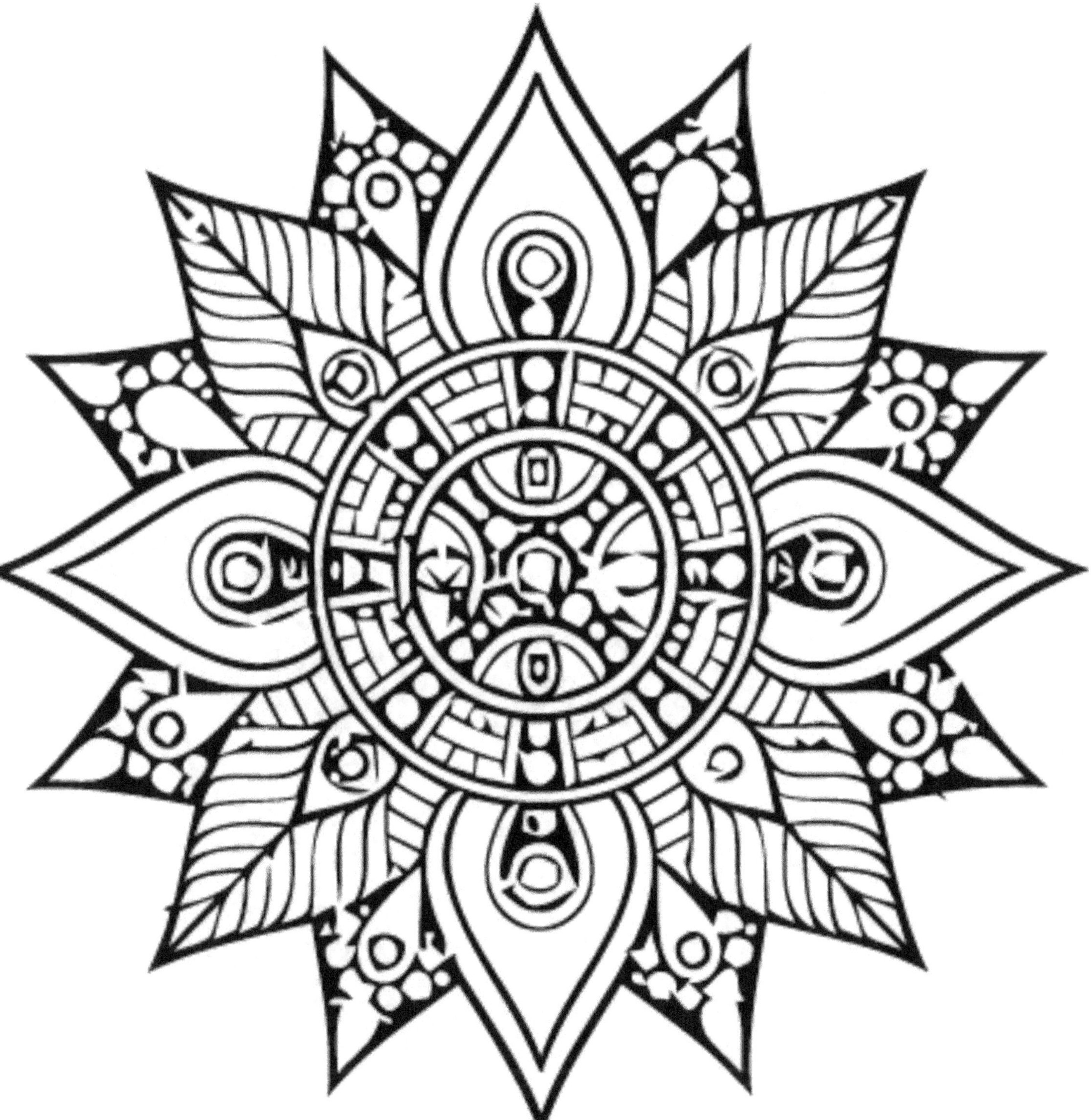

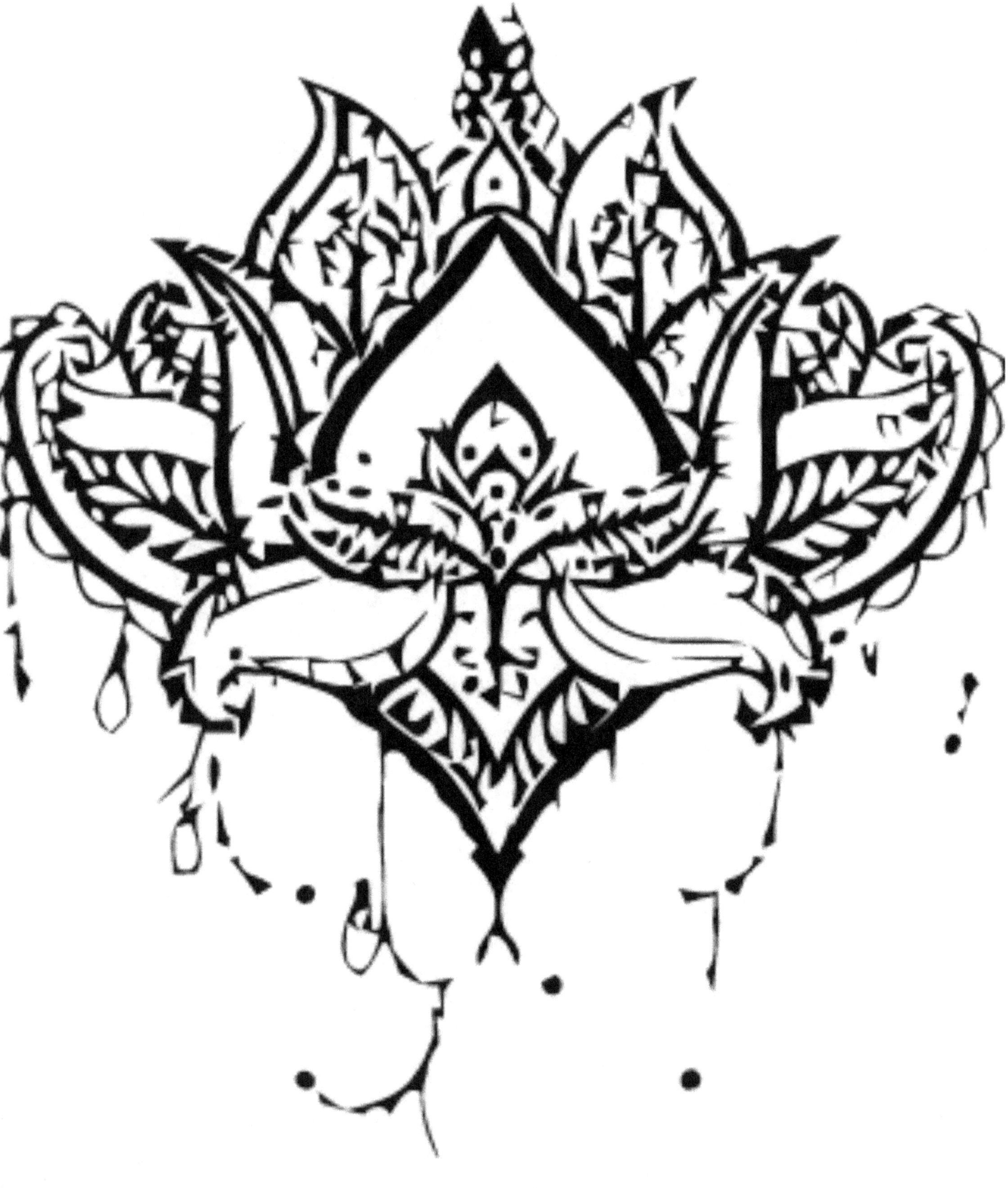

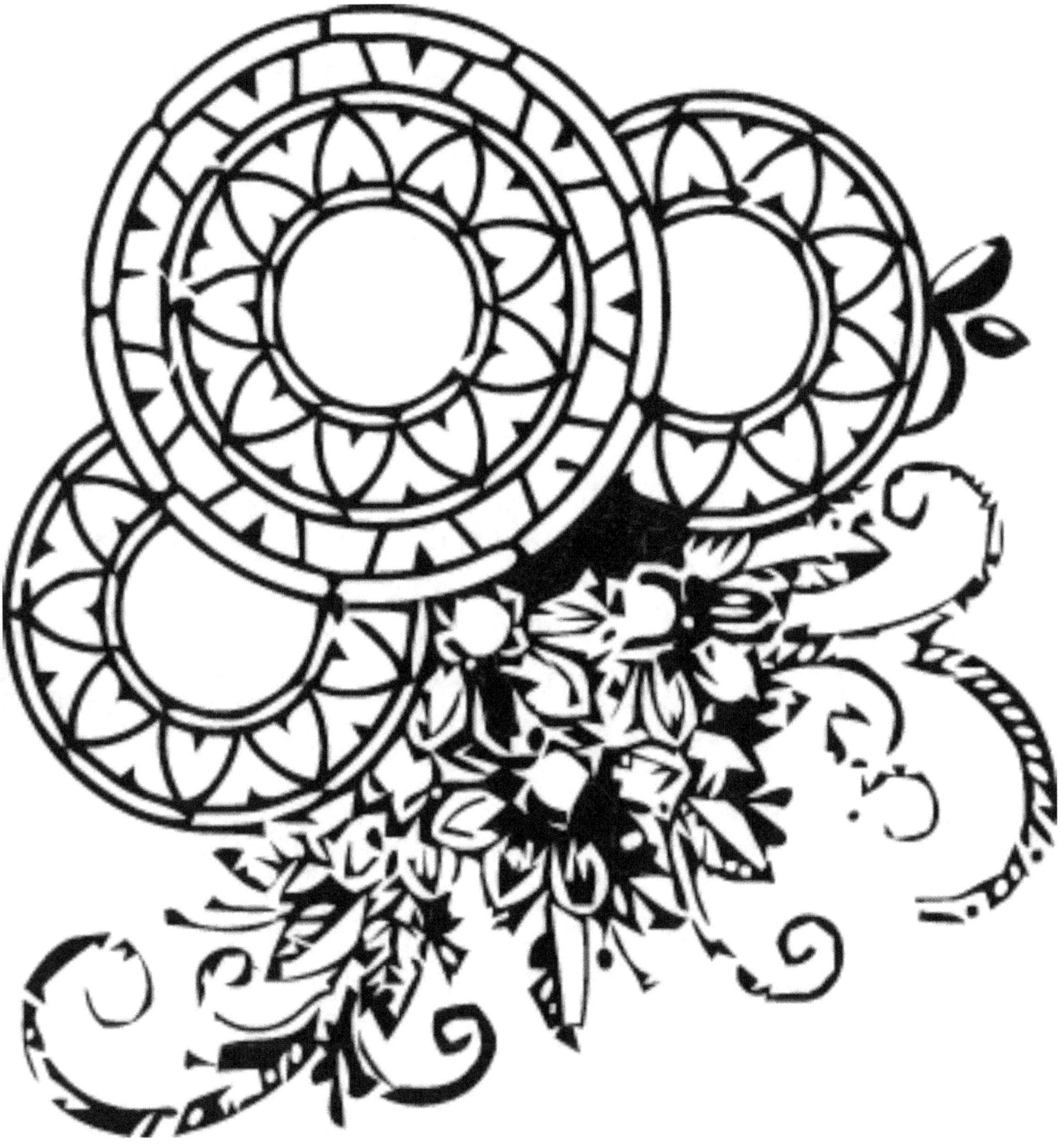

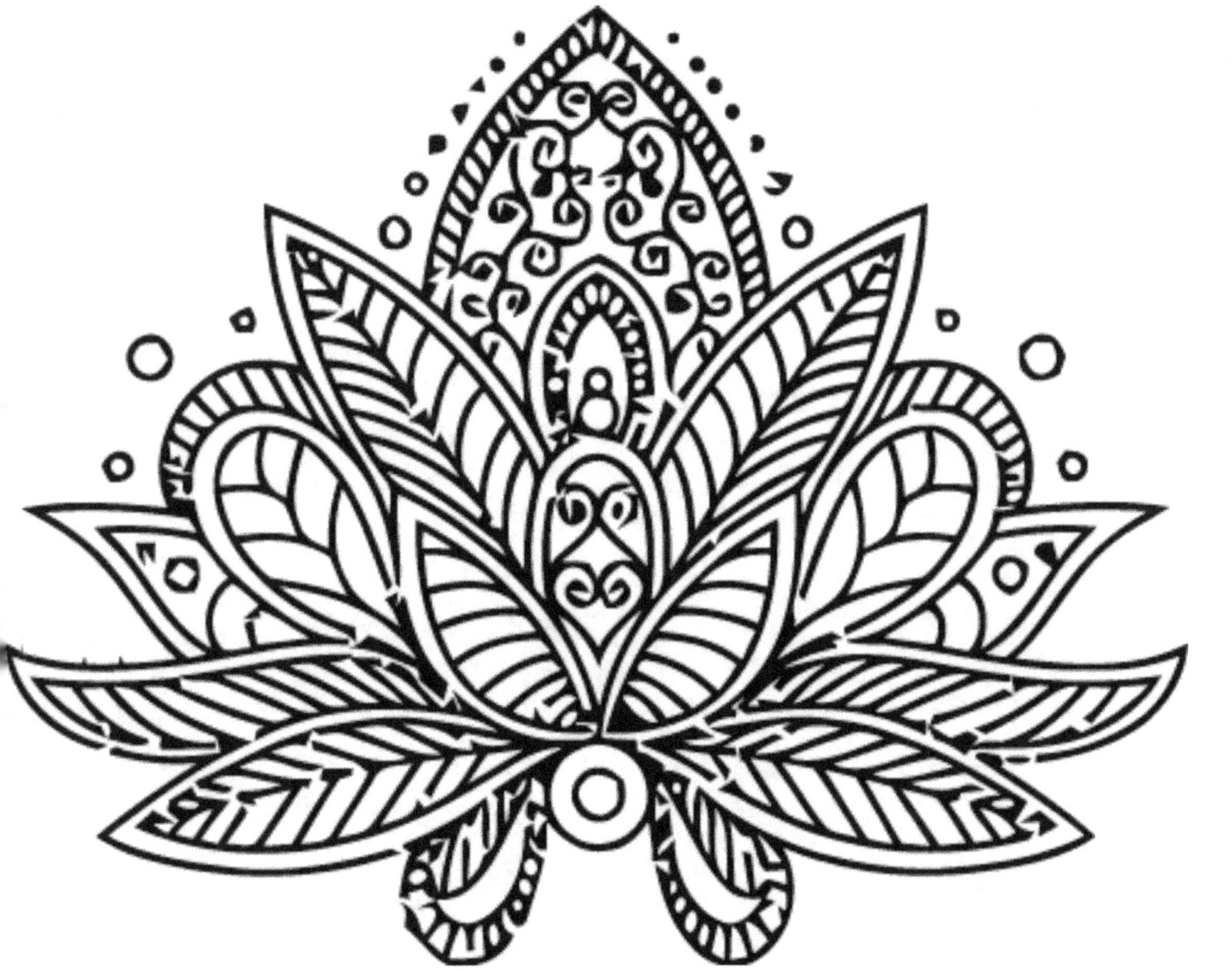

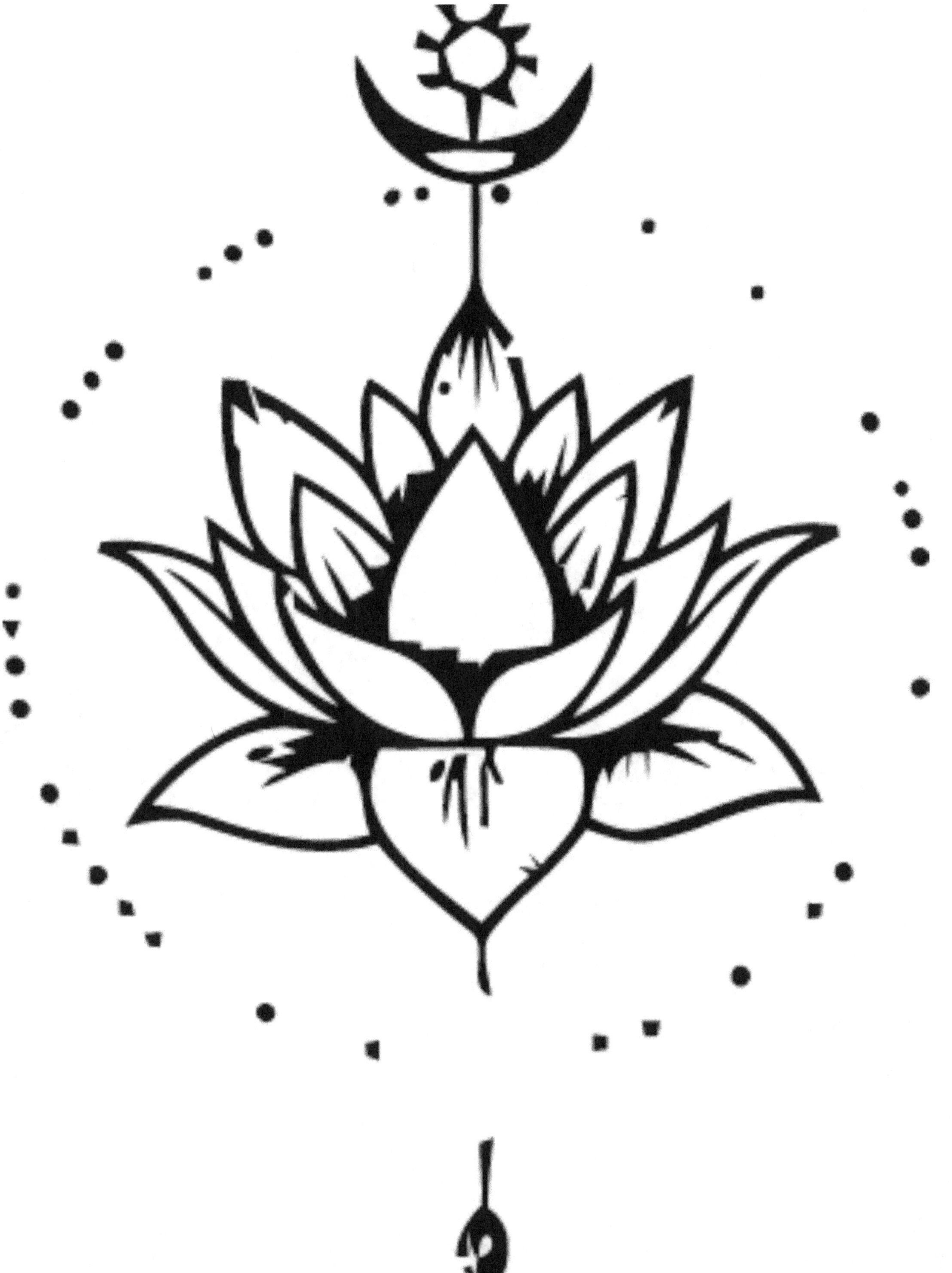

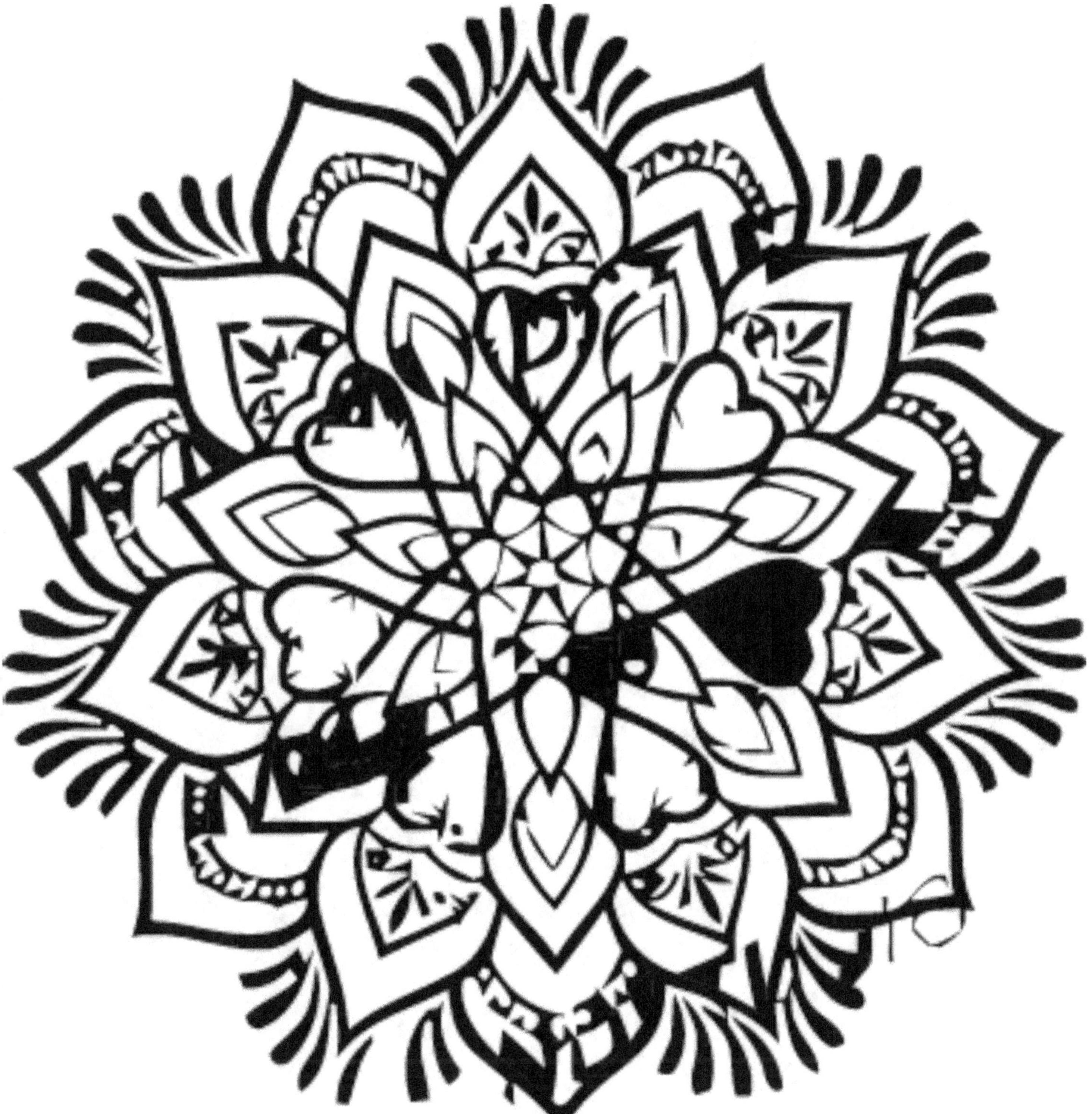

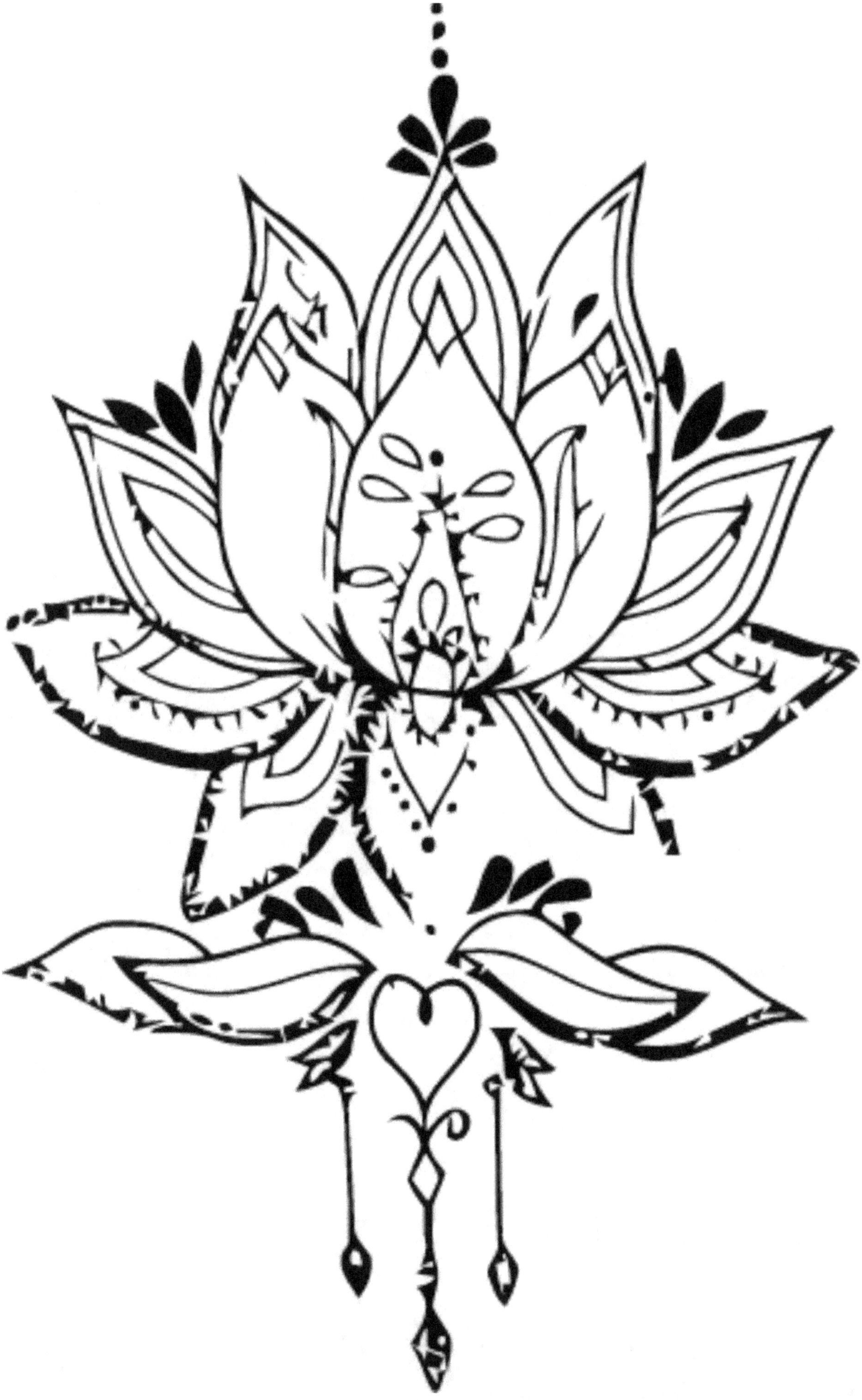

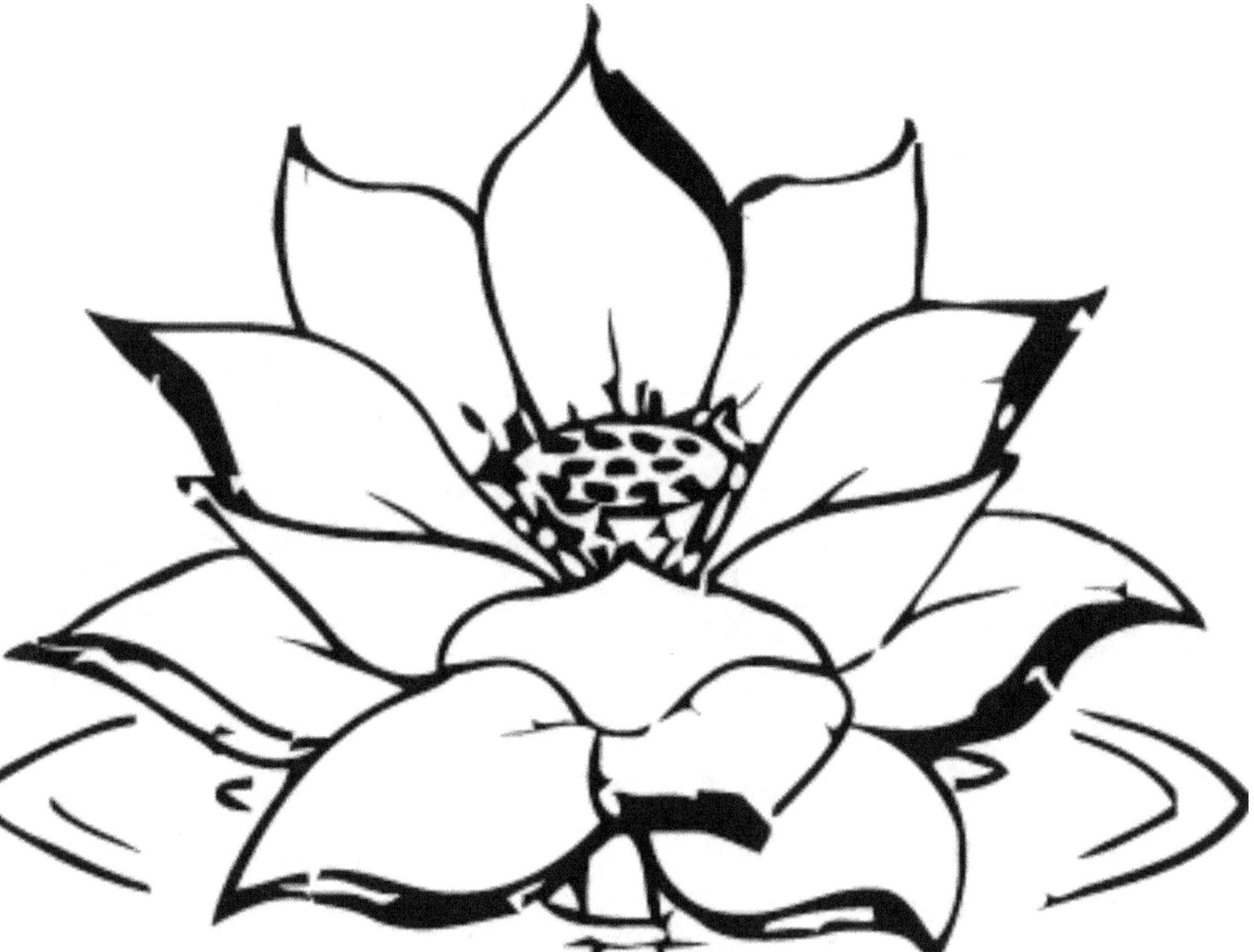

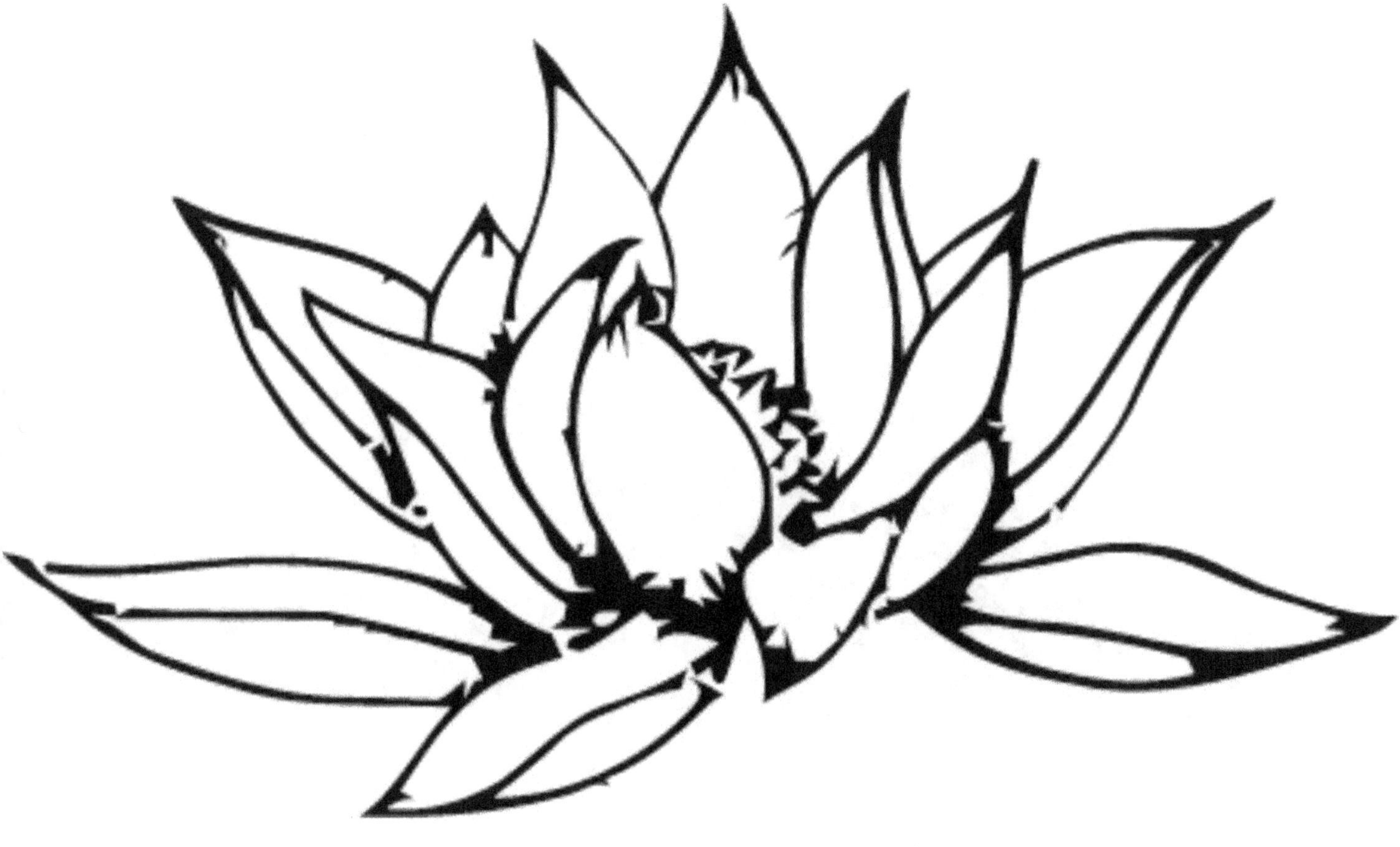

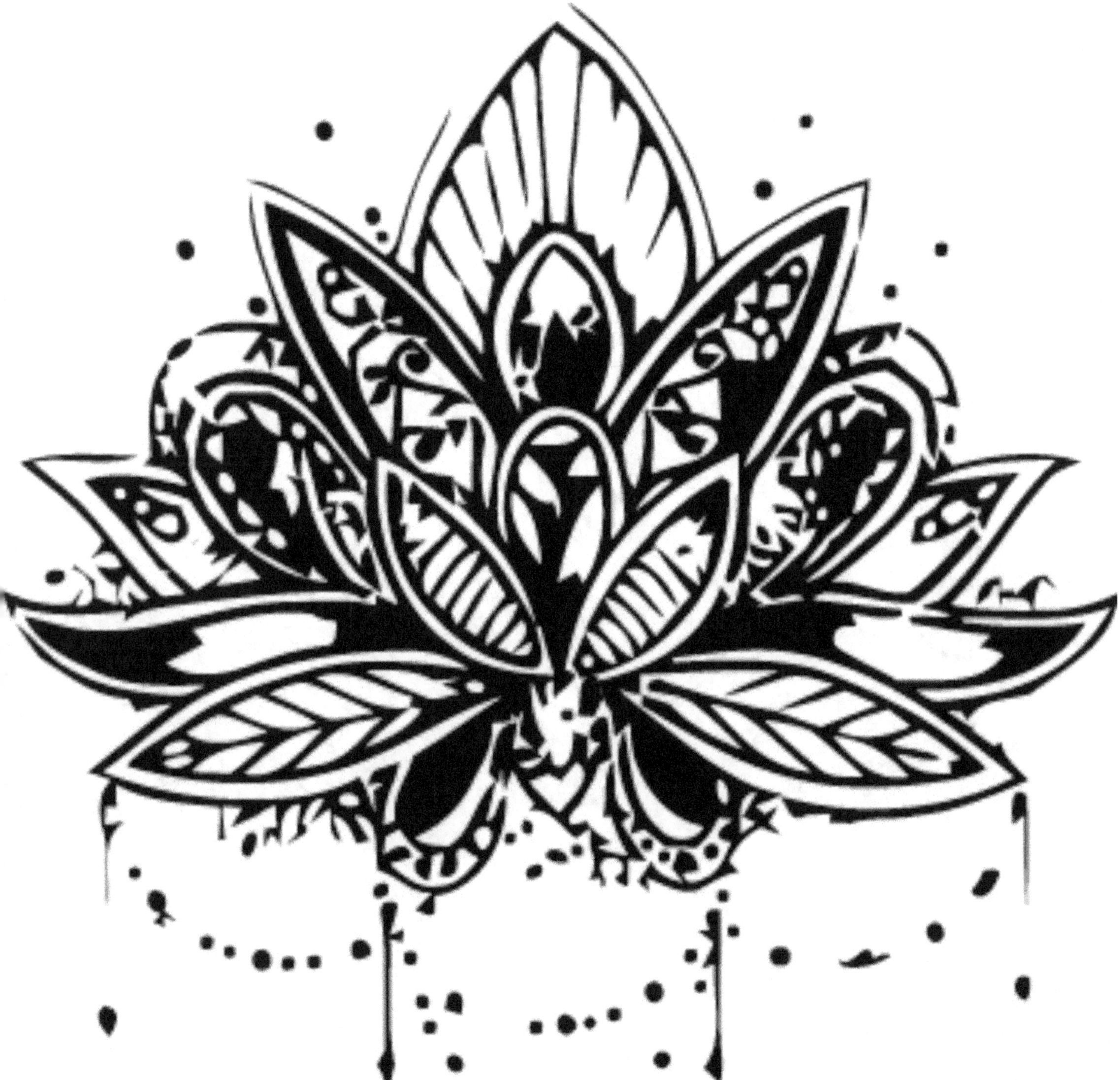

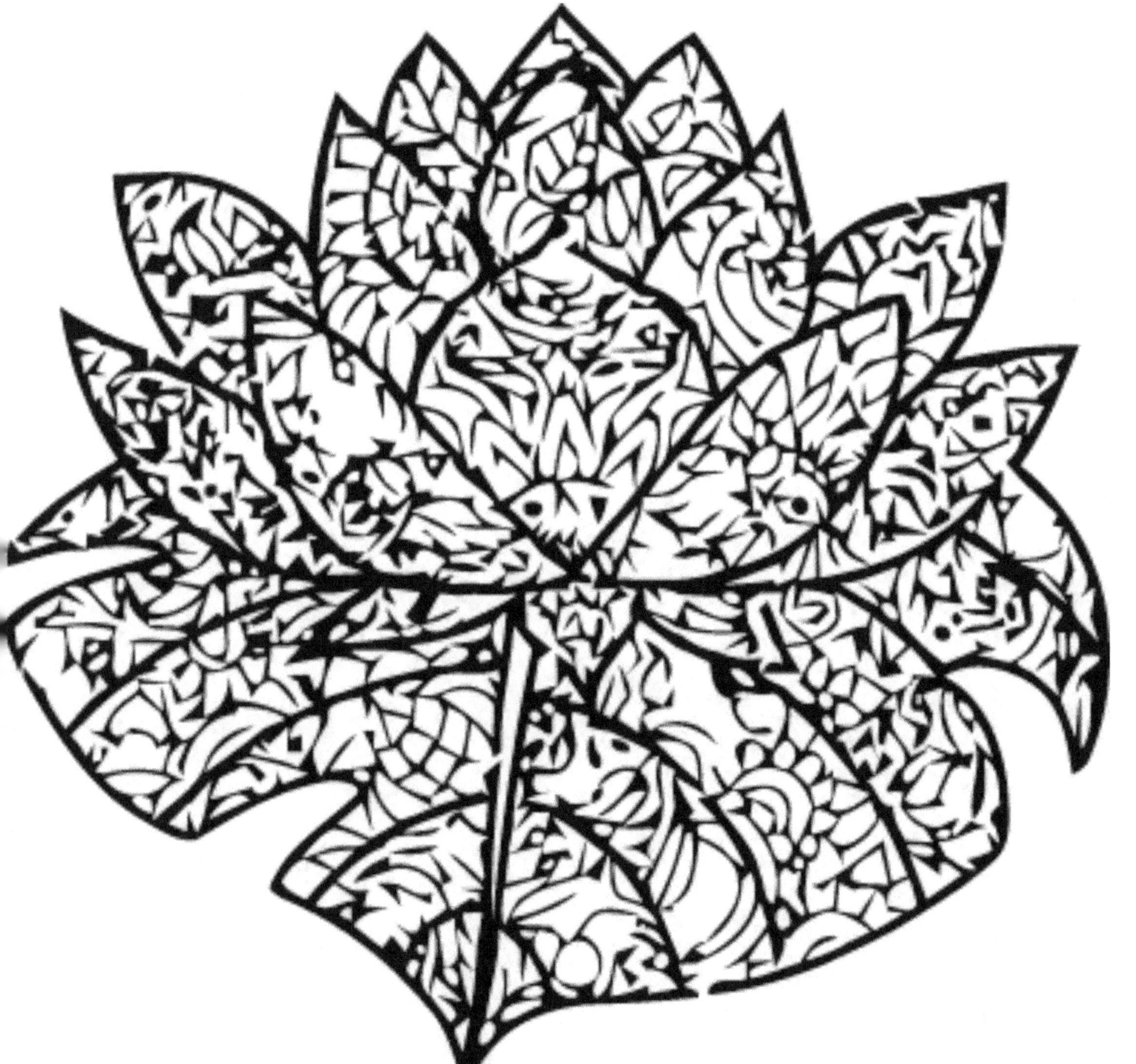

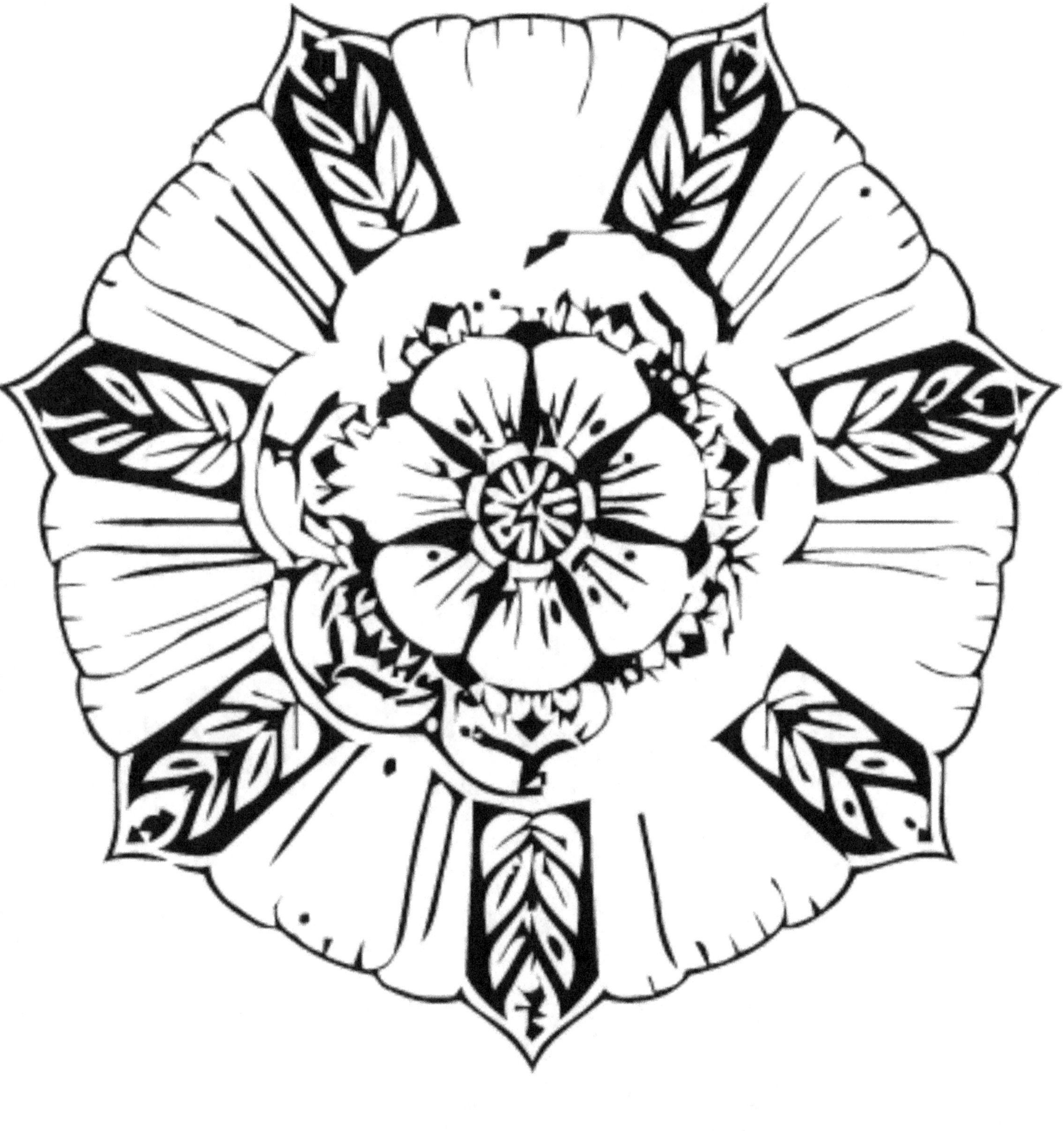

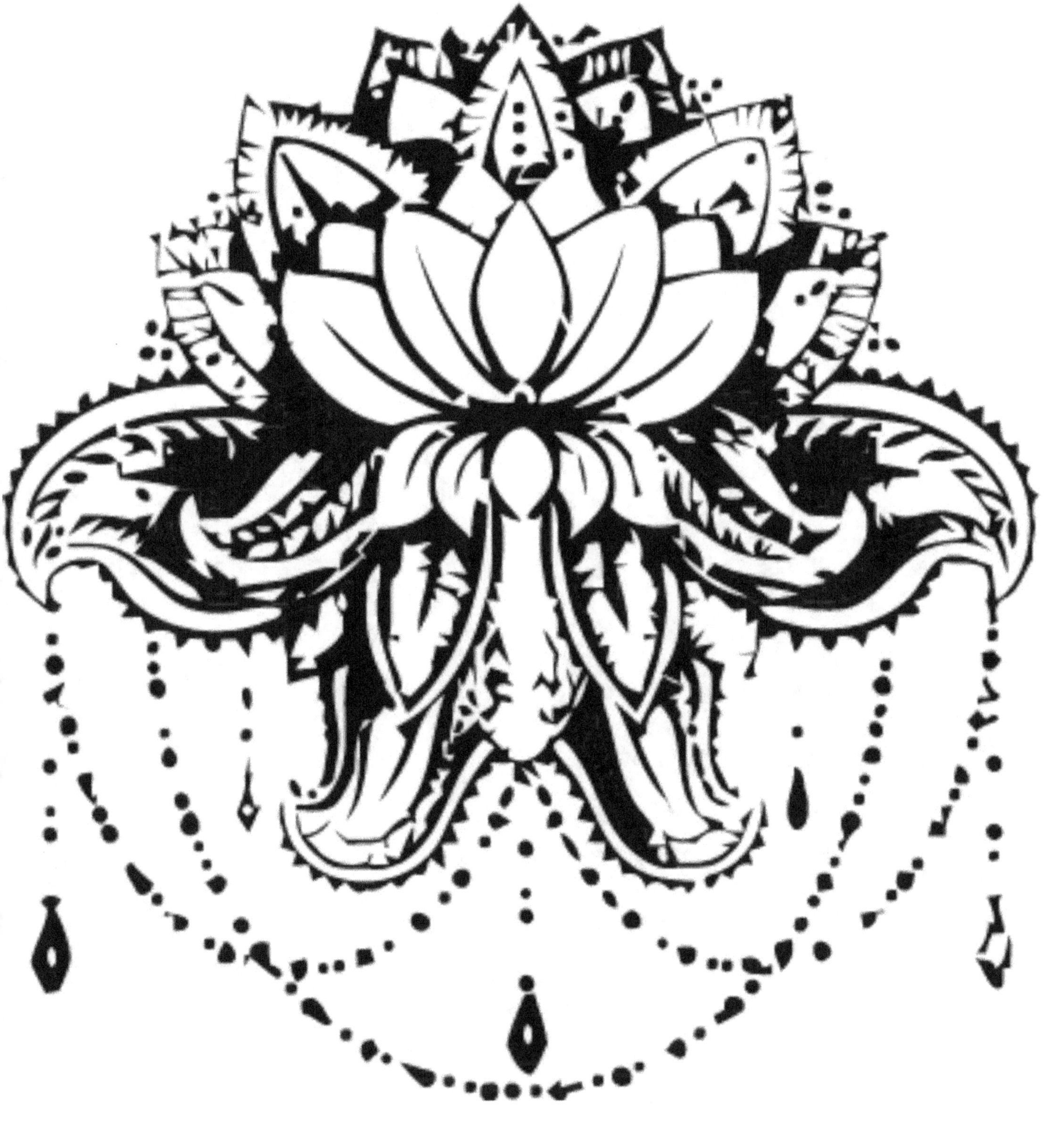

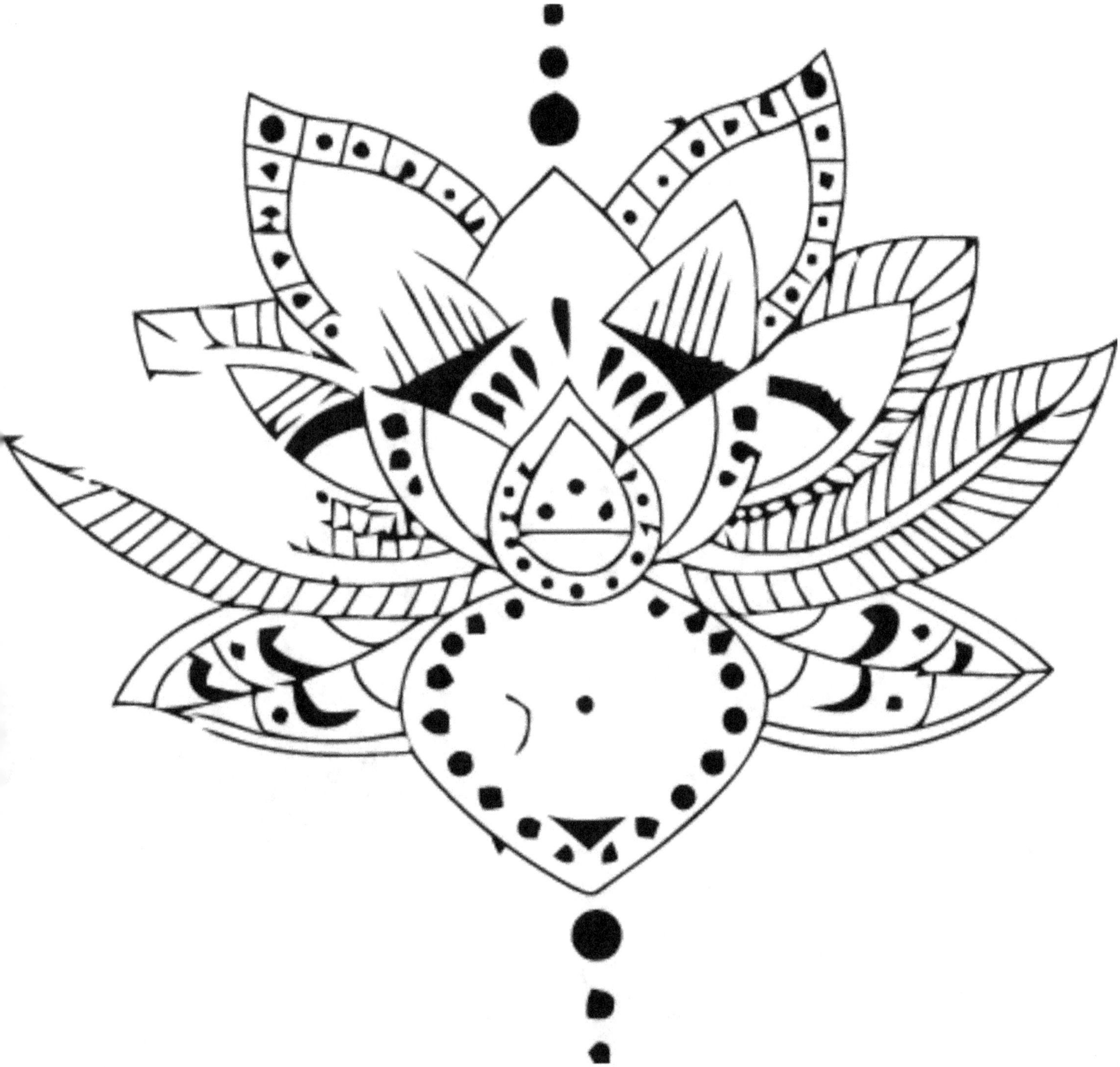

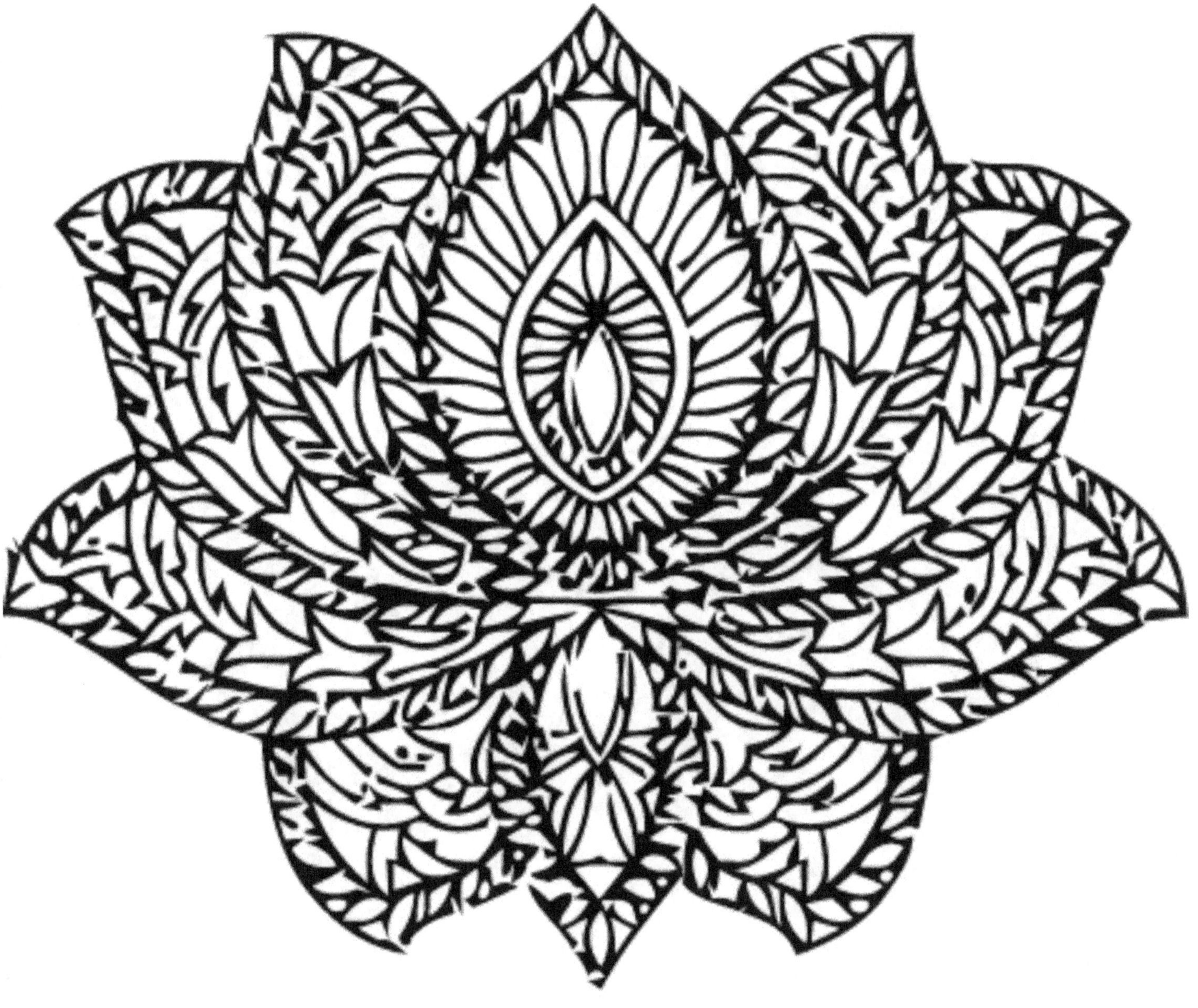

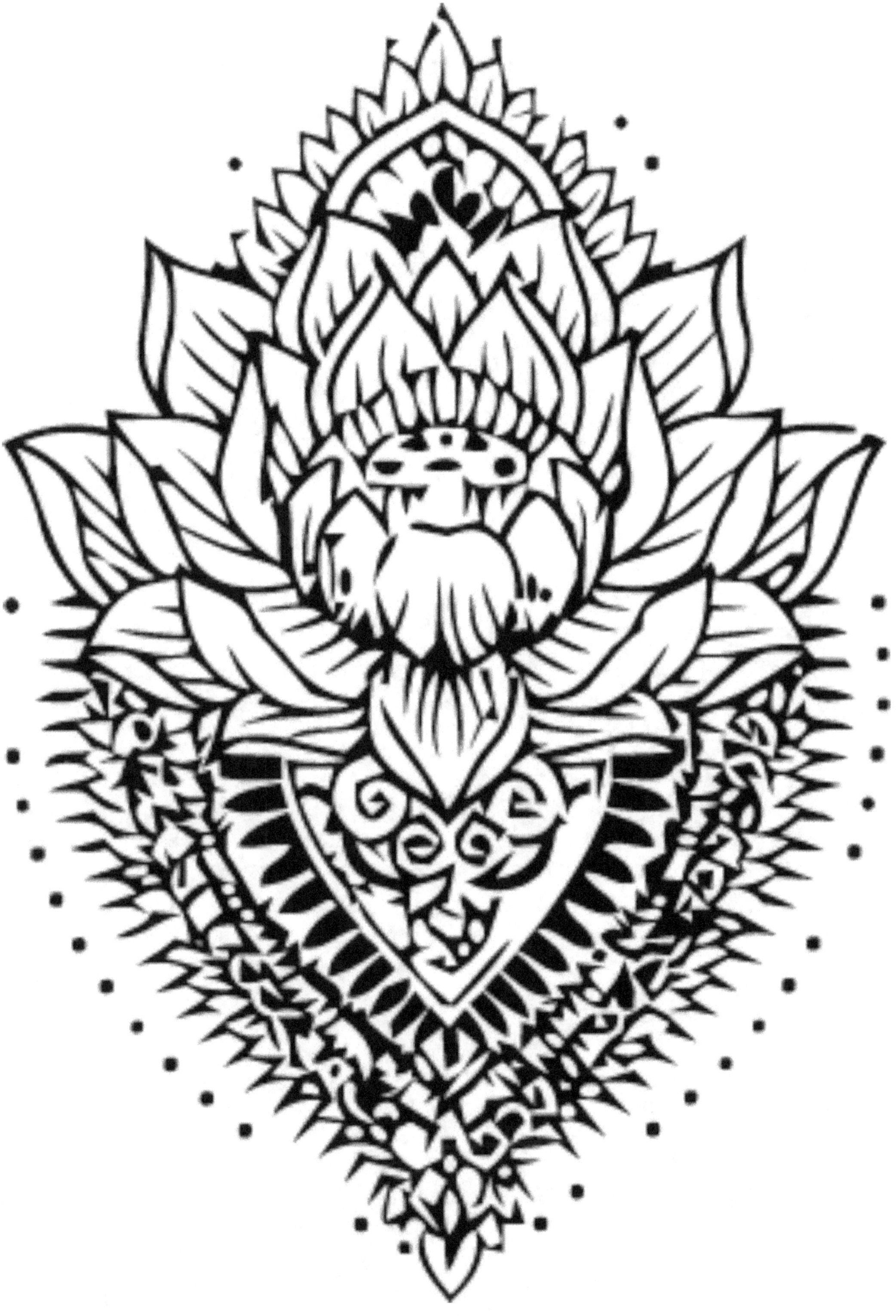

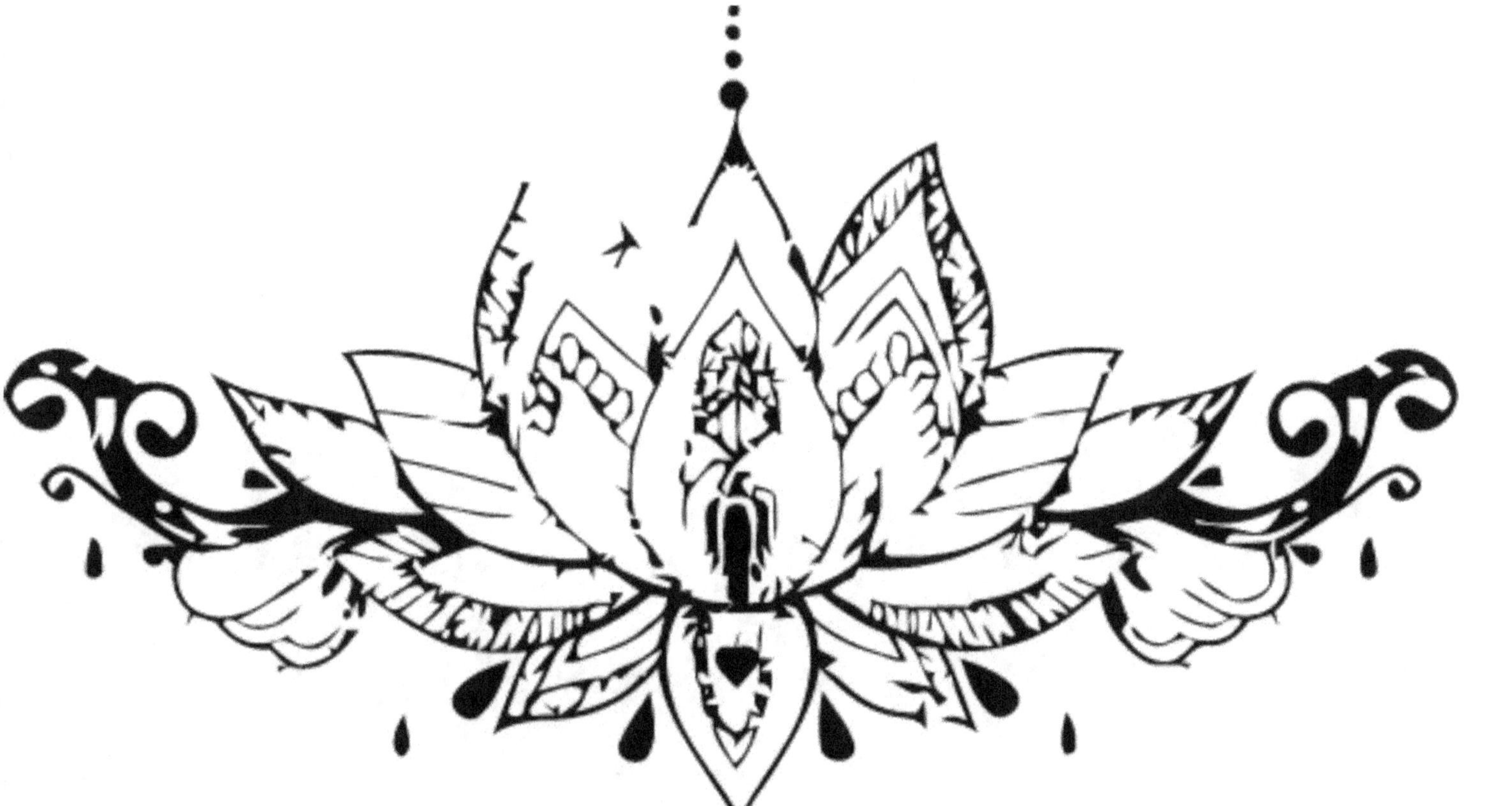

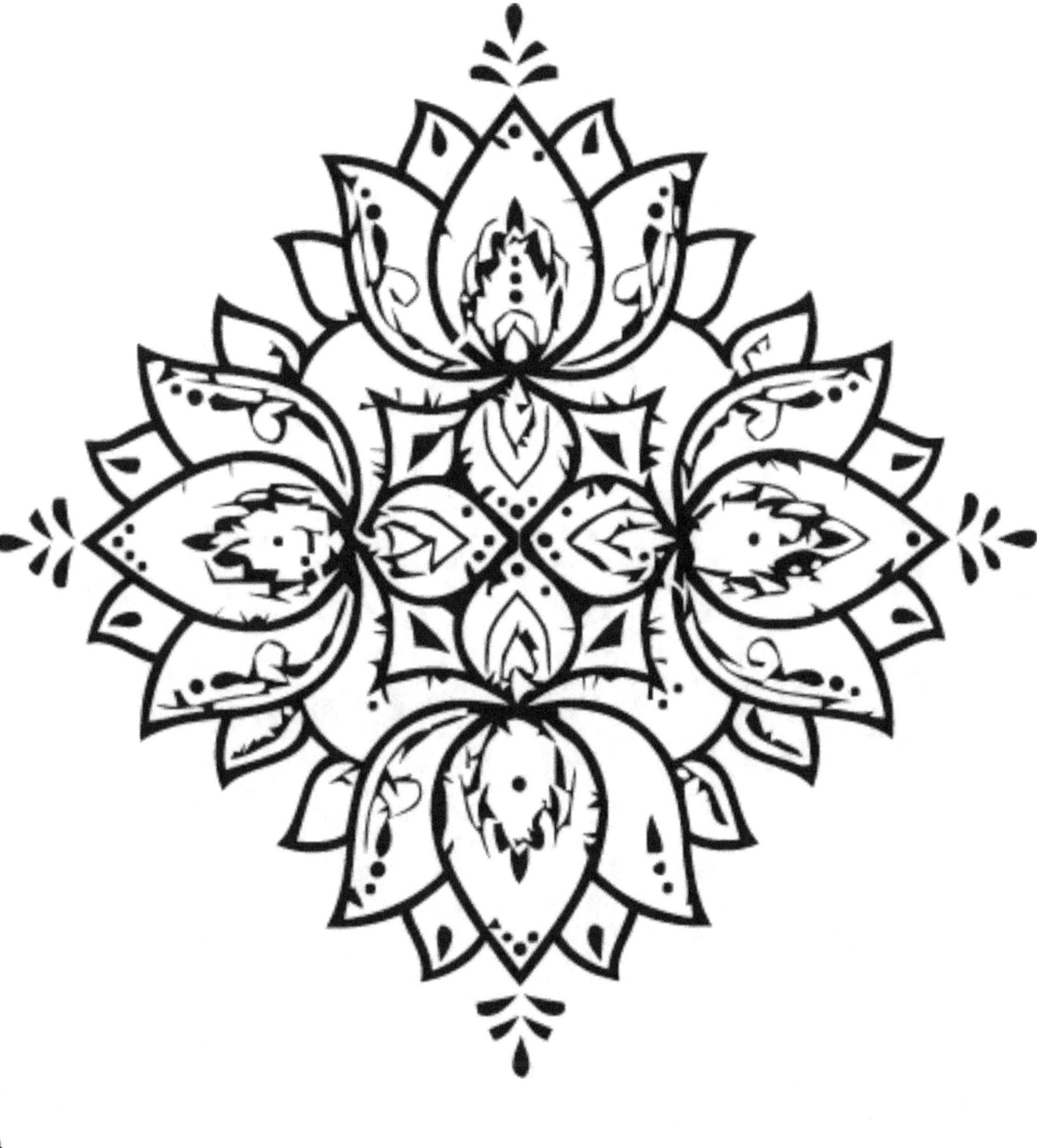

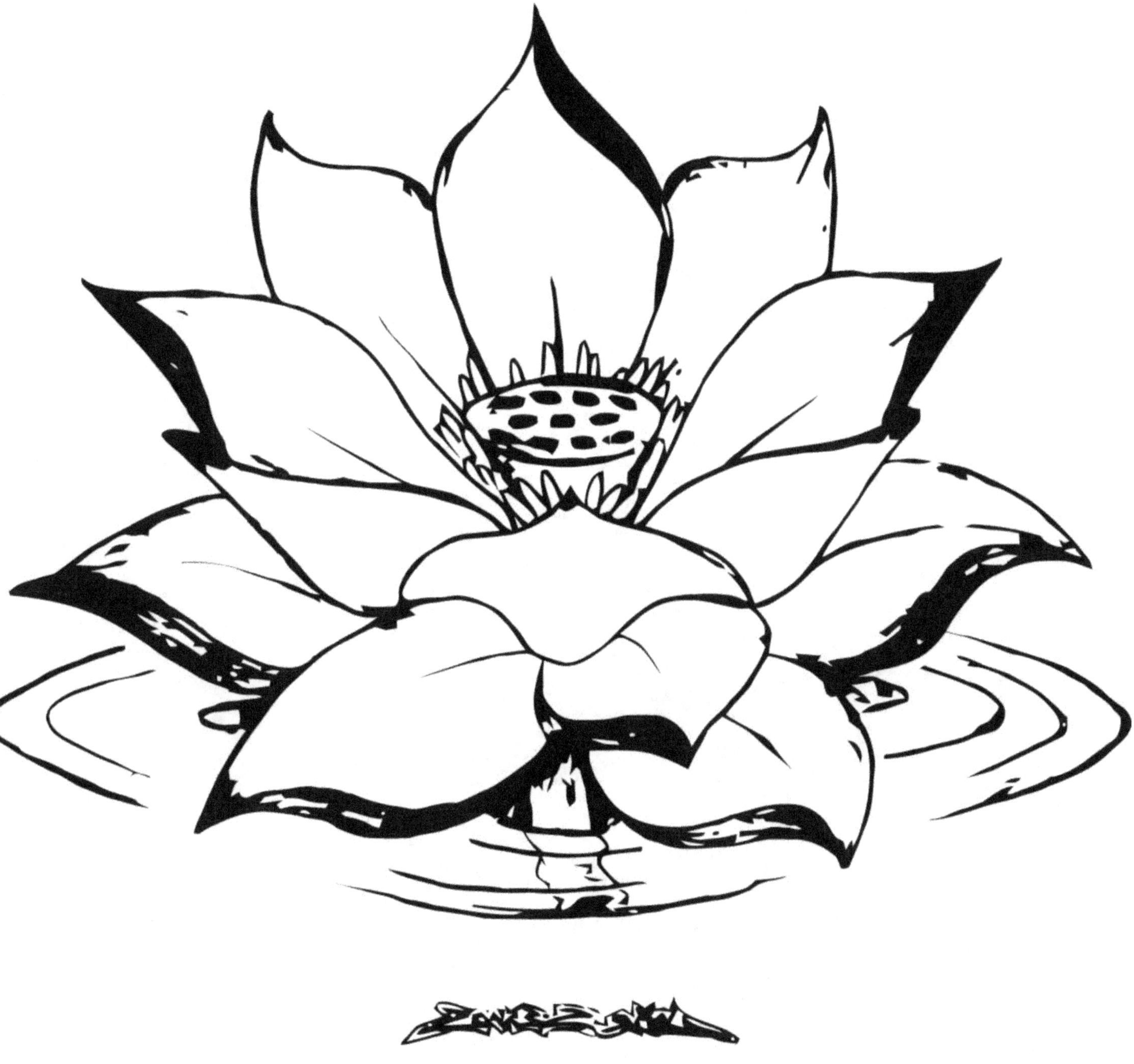

www.ingramcontent.com/pod-product-compliance
Lightning Source LLC
Chambersburg PA
CBHW080519220526
45465CB00006B/2534
* 9 7 9 8 6 3 0 2 1 1 4 4 6 *